WITHDRAWN

BEHIND
THE BADGE

CRIMEFIGHTERS THROUGH HISTORY

ED BUTTS
ART BY GARETH WILLIAMS

annick press
toronto + new york + vancouver

Edited by Pam Robertson
Copyedited by Linda Pruessen
Proofread by Catherine Marjoribanks
Additional Illustrations © Caitlin Bauman
Designed by Caitlin Bauman Design & Illustration

Annick Press Ltd.

We acknowledge the support of the Canada Council for the Arts, the Ontario Arts Council, and the Government of Canada through the Canada Book Fund (CBF) for our publishing activities.

Cataloging in Publication

Butts, Edward, 1951-, author
    Behind the badge : crime fighters through history / Ed Butts ; art by Gareth Williams.

Includes bibliographical references and index.
ISBN 978-1-55451-675-9 (bound).--ISBN 978-1-55451-674-2 (pbk.)

    1. Police--History--Juvenile literature. 2. Law enforcement--History--Juvenile literature. 3. Crime prevention--History--Juvenile literature. I. Williams, Gareth Glyn, illustrator II. Title.

HV7922.B88 2014   j363.209   C2014-900614-4

Distributed in Canada by:
Firefly Books Ltd.
50 Staples Avenue, Unit 1
Richmond Hill, ON L4B 0A7

Published in the U.S.A. by Annick Press (U.S.) Ltd.
Distributed in the U.S.A. by:
Firefly Books (U.S.) Inc.
P.O. Box 1338 Ellicott Station
Buffalo, NY 14205

Printed in China

Visit us at: www.annickpress.com

Also available in e-book format. Please visit www.annickpress.com/ebooks.html for more details. Or scan

TABLE OF CONTENTS

TO THE MEN AND WOMEN IN UNIFORM
WHO SERVE WITH HONOR AND DO THEIR
BEST TO KEEP THE PUBLIC SAFE—EB

TO RENÉ, MOM, DAD,
WARREN AND MA ANSIE—GW

INTRODUCTION

THIS BOOK TAKES YOU ON A JOURNEY. IT IS A JOURNEY WHERE you will learn what it was like to patrol dark, crime-infested streets alone at night. You will see how new inventions like streetlights revolutionized police work. You'll meet the many people who are part of the world of law and law enforcement: political leaders, magistrates, crime victims, and criminals. You'll also discover what it takes to be a police officer today, see how modern police work to prevent crime, and learn about the latest methods used to solve crimes.

Imagine what it would be like if you had to worry about being attacked or run over as you rode your bike down the street. It's not hard to picture how an everyday experience could become extremely dangerous without laws to maintain order. But if there were no agents to enforce those laws, they would be pointless. That's why police are among the most vital members of our communities. They carry enormous responsibility—protecting lives and property and ensuring that citizens feel safe. It's true that they are crime fighters, but they also work at keeping the peace, resolving conflict, and preventing crime.

WHAT IS THE ORIGIN OF THE WORD *POLICE*?

Words like *police, policy,* and *politics* all stem from the Greek word *politeia*, which means "state" or "government." The French-speaking Norman invaders introduced the word *policie* (civil organization) to England. The first official use of the word *police* in English was in 1714, when Queen Anne appointed several nobles to be Commissioners of Police in Scotland.

Thanks to movies, television, and video games, we often think about police in terms of dramatic episodes—car chases and bloody shoot-outs—but moments like these actually make up a small percentage of police work. More typically, police respond to every-day events—they patrol city streets and rural highways, control traffic, respond to emergencies, and are on hand to provide security for large gatherings.

That doesn't mean the work is easy. On the contrary, policing is complex. The job covers a vast range of duties, from finding lost children and intervening in domestic disturbances to conducting undercover drug operations and tackling crime-solving forensic investigations. Police provide a public service that frequently requires sophisticated problem-solving skills and quick thinking.

All societies need a way to maintain order, and as society changes, so does the nature of crime. Not so long ago, no one had heard of cybercrime. Yet today, police devote considerable staff time and other resources to fighting Internet lawbreakers. In short, policing is a constantly evolving role, even though the fundamentals of ensuring the public sense of security remain unchanged.

Bygone societies didn't have police departments as we know them now. So how did people of other times and places enforce

---

WHY ARE POLICE CALLED *COPS*?

The word *cop* might have come from the Latin verb *capere* or the Anglo-Saxon verb *coppe*, both meaning "to catch" or "to take." The word *copper* has been a slang term for police in the British Isles for over three hundred years. Some people incorrectly believe cop is an acronym for "constable on patrol."

laws and protect themselves from criminals? Who were the first police? How did police evolve over the centuries into the specially trained professionals of the 21st century who stand as the front line against crime?

In the prehistoric world, and in some more recent but isolated societies, chiefs and warriors enforced community laws. Some ancient rulers relied on soldiers to keep order and apprehend criminals. In one Greek city, the police were slaves. As civilizations grew and became more complex, policing methods evolved. An English sheriff in the medieval period would call upon peasant farmers to form a posse and pursue a lawbreaker. In China, officials called prefects enforced the law with the aid of retired soldiers.

If we could put together a picture gallery of police from across the ages, the many images would include the urban cohorts of Imperial Rome, a Japanese samurai warrior, a member of the Watch from Elizabethan London, a marshal from the American Wild West, and a modern-day city constable—dramatically different in their appearance and their roles, but all serving the same basic purpose.

Police haven't always just upheld laws against crimes like robbery and murder. In different times and places they have been fire-control officers, dress-code enforcers, and even gardeners. They have enforced religious rules and social regulations that seem strange to people today. The police in some societies were objects of considerable fear and mistrust because their main duty was to spy on people and root out anyone they considered a threat to their monarch or dictator. Sadly, there have also been (and continue to be) instances in which the police have been guilty of criminal acts.

THE WORLD OF POLICING

Laws, courts, trials, fines, and jail are designed to compel people to obey the law. Once upon a time, people were afraid to break the law because they thought the gods were watching them. Today people are often watched by surveillance cameras, which are used to discourage crime in areas with high foot and vehicle traffic. Even something as simple as a speed bump on a road helps to keep people from violating traffic regulations.

CHAPTER 1

THE PREHISTORIC WORLD:
CHIEFS, CAMP POLICE, AND ELDERS

LOOKING INTO THE ROOTS OF POLICING HAS ITS CHALLENGES.
Humans didn't begin to develop writing until about 3200 BCE.
The long period of time before that is known as the prehistoric era.
We know that people in prehistoric societies had to work together
to survive—cooperation was essential for a successful hunt or a
bountiful harvest. We also know that cooperation would have been
impossible without rules. Societies established systems of rules so
everybody would know what their responsibilities were, and to
ensure that people lived together in harmony. But because those
early people left no records, we don't know what the rules were
or who enforced them.

However, we do have insights into that distant world. Some
very old societies survived and thrived for centuries in isolation,
away from the influence of the literate world. Starting in the 15th
century, Europeans first began to probe the regions of the world
that were unknown to them. Since then, explorers, missionaries,
and adventurers—and, more recently, scientists and other scholars—
have encountered diverse peoples living as their ancestors did for
thousands of years. Their recorded observations of age-old traditions
give us a picture of what "policing" might have been like in the
prehistoric world.

FIRST NATIONS OF THE AMERICAS

Many nations, differing in cultures and languages, make up the Native population of North and South America. Before the arrival of Europeans, they all had their own laws. There were also people in each tribe or nation who were responsible for enforcing the rules.

Councils of prominent men governed Huron villages in what is now central Canada. They judged people accused of serious crimes such as murder and witchcraft. A person found guilty might be allowed to compensate for the offense by giving gifts to the victim or the victim's family. Otherwise, the punishment was exile.

One of the most important community activities of the Illinois nation, who lived along the upper Mississippi River, was the buffalo hunt. Young warriors took turns serving as camp police, ensuring that everyone did whatever was necessary for the hunt to be successful. They destroyed the property of anyone whose irresponsible behavior jeopardized the hunt.

The Atsugewi of western North America paid *shamans* (magicians or medicine men) to find thieves. The chief could request, but not demand, the return of stolen property. The relatives of a murder victim could kill the murderer, or they could force him to support the victim's family.

In the Maidu nation's territory, which is now part of northern California, all lands and waters were divided up among villages for hunting and fishing rights. Men worked in pairs to guard the boundaries, preventing villagers from poaching each other's fish and game. These boundary police were chosen for their good judgement and steadiness of temper. Their badge of office was a single magpie feather worn upright on top of the head.

The Inca of Peru, the Aztecs of Mexico, and the Maya of southern Mexico and Central America all had advanced civilizations before the arrival of Europeans in the 16th century. They built cities, expanded into empires, and ruled with codes of law. It's hard to know what aspects of their laws originated in prehistoric times, but when we consider how much these civilizations resembled those of early Europe and the Middle East, it's reasonable to conclude that their rules evolved from a tribal period lost in the mists of time.

Incan law was simple. It forbade laziness, adultery, theft, and murder. Inspectors known as *tokoyrikoq* (one who sees all) spied on everyone. A woman who didn't keep her house clean could be arrested just the same as a man caught stealing a neighbor's llama or cheating on his taxes. The town of Tambo had the official responsibility of providing the empire's constables. When the Incan army conquered a new territory, the inhabitants were forced to move to different parts of the empire so they couldn't organize a rebellion. It was one of the Incan constables' duties to make sure the dispersed people didn't return home.

In Aztec society much of the "policing" was done by clan groups called *calpullis*. They ensured that people obeyed the laws against such unacceptable behavior as public drunkenness. The calpullis were answerable to official representatives of the emperor. Merchants called *pochteca* controlled Aztec marketplaces. They hired men to serve as police, watching for thieves and dishonest vendors.

We don't know who actually did the policing in Mayan society. However, we do know that criminals were among those who were sacrificed to the gods by Mayan priests, and people who displeased the king were severely punished. It's very likely that warriors or village headmen apprehended wrongdoers and turned them over to higher authorities for judgement.

CRIME REPORT

Cocoa beans (also called cacao beans), from which chocolate is made, were so valuable in Aztec society that they were used as money. The police in Aztec marketplaces had to watch for dishonest shoppers and merchants who made counterfeit beans by filling empty rinds with sawdust.

When European explorers first reached the Hawaiian Islands in the 18th century, the native Hawaiians were living under an ancient legal and religious code called *kapu*. Kapu governed every aspect of daily life, from how to prepare food to how to construct a canoe. Certain foods were forbidden to women, and fishing was allowed only at specified times of the year. Common people had to kneel in the presence of a king or chief, and never, ever allow their shadow to fall upon the body of such a revered person. Only kings, chiefs, and priests were allowed to wear certain feathers. The penalty for breaking any rule of kapu, even by accident, was death. Chiefs, sub-chiefs, and warriors enforced the rules of kapu. A person who violated the law had just one way to escape immediate execution: running to a place that was considered sacred ground and claiming the protection of the gods.

The Maori people of New Zealand, like the native Hawaiians, are Polynesian. European explorers found that the Maori were governed by a code called *tapu* that was very

A MISUNDERSTANDING?

In 1779, Hawaiian warriors killed the English explorer Captain James Cook. The English had previously been on good terms with the natives, but unknowingly broke a rule of kapu by overstaying their welcome. The situation deteriorated when Cook attempted to take a chief hostage to force the Hawaiians to return a stolen boat. Laying hands on a chief was another violation of kapu. Captain Cook was clubbed and stabbed to death.

similar to kapu. Maori also lived according to a sense of personal honor called *mana*. A man called a *tohunga* (spiritual leader) was responsible for enforcing the rules. There were physical penalties, including death, for transgressors. However, the Maori believed the most terrible punishments would come from the gods.

There is strong evidence that elders were the law enforcers in prehistoric communities. They were often revered because of the experience and wisdom they'd gained through their long lives, and younger people respected their decisions. Among people who had no written legal codes, these elders understood traditional laws better than anyone else. Australia and Africa provide us with good examples of societies in which law enforcement by elders lasted from a time in the dim past until well into the modern age.

Among the aboriginal peoples of Australia, elders conducted inquests and decided if a lawbreaker should be executed or exiled. If the offender was a man, they might sentence him to stand with only a small shield for protection while other men threw spears and boomerangs at him. Often, the ordeal ended as soon as blood was drawn.

PEACE OFFICERS

The murder of an Australian Aborigine could result in "payback" killings and long blood feuds. Sometimes rival groups met on "law grounds" so leaders could negotiate an end to a feud.

Chiefs and male elders were also the senior authorities among the Zulu people of South Africa. They made the important decisions and disciplined anyone who broke the rules.

Under the great 19th-century Zulu king Shaka, the punishment for just about any breach of the rules was death. After Shaka's assassination, Zulu law became less drastic.

In a Zulu village, the chief's eldest sons performed a type of policing role as official gatekeepers. Armed with spears and shields, they stood guard at the village gate. They turned away anyone who was not welcome. Visitors who were granted entry were escorted to the chief's home, and the gatekeepers sang their father's praises. Gatekeeping was part of the training for youths who would one day be chiefs.

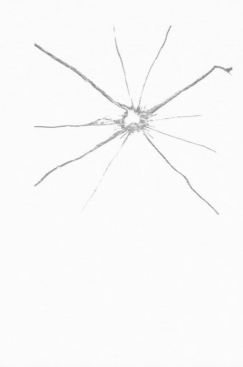

CHAPTER 2

LAW AND ORDER IN THE ANCIENT WORLD

THE PERIOD OF DOCUMENTED HISTORY WE CALL "ANCIENT" BEGAN about 3500 BCE with the rise of civilizations in fertile river valleys of Mesopotamia, Egypt, India, and China. People learned to make metal tools and weapons, and developed systems of writing. Agricultural communities and trading centers grew into cities. That called for more complex systems of government, and rules for large numbers of people living and working together. Old traditional laws that varied from one village to another were no longer adequate. The new civilizations required laws that applied to everyone.

The earliest known code of law was written by Hammurabi, king of Babylon. Hammurabi's Code (c. 1772 BCE) was heavily based on religion. The Babylonians believed that the gods were always watching, and would punish them in this world or the next for any wrongdoing. That was a strong incentive for people to obey the law, but Hammurabi knew that it wouldn't work for everyone. He administered justice according to the policy of "an eye for an eye, and a tooth for a tooth." Whatever wrong a person did to another would be paid back in kind. A boy who struck his father could have a hand or some fingers cut off. A man who didn't pay his debts could be sold into slavery, along with his wife and children.

Hammurabi would have had a flesh-and-blood law enforcement team of soldiers and priests. They did the gods' work in apprehending and punishing offenders. But they weren't police. Many centuries passed before official police units appeared in the ancient world.

THE SCYTHIAN ARCHERS OF ATHENS

In 355 BCE, the government of Athens, Greece, cracked down on tax evaders. Backed by a squad of police, an official named Androtion entered the homes of the wealthy and confiscated undeclared riches. He arrested tax dodgers, and his police took them to jail to be held for trial. Who were those "police"?

In most ancient civilizations, soldiers kept order. Athens was one of the most powerful of the Greek city-states, and the birthplace of democratic government. It was also the first city known to have a body of men specifically authorized to be police. They were called the Scythian Archers.

The Scythians were a fierce nomadic people who inhabited the region northeast of the Black Sea. Their skill with the bow and arrow was legendary. Athenians colonized areas around the Black Sea, and it's likely that Scythians arrived in Athens as prisoners of war. In the 5th century BCE, a politician named Speusinos organized them into a force of city guards. It was common in those times for a powerful state to force captives to fight in its army, so the idea of using state-owned slaves as police wasn't as odd as it might seem now. Actually, using foreigners as police was logical to the Athenians, who didn't like the idea of Greeks arresting fellow Greeks.

The Scythian Archers patrolled the streets at night, guarded the city gates and other important locations, and kept order in the Agora, the main marketplace. They carried whips that they used to keep public places clear of vagrants, drunkards, and rowdies. In times of war, when thousands of refugees from the countryside poured intoAthens seeking the safety of its walls, the Scythian Archers were used for crowd control. All those extra people strained the city's facilities and resources, creating an enormous potential for trouble in the streets.

The Scythian Archers didn't investigate crimes. If you were robbed, or if someone in your family was murdered, you had to conduct your own investigation.

ANCIENT SURVEILLANCE

In the city-state of Sparta, slaves called *helots* did all of the agricultural work. A police force of Spartan youth called the *krypteia* spied on the helots to discourage revolt. The krypteia could kill a helot just for being outside his hut after dark.

If you came up with a suspect, you reported that person to the Assembly, the Athenian government. The Assembly would then call the suspect to come and face you, the accuser. If the suspect failed to respond to the summons, the Assembly sent the Scythian Archers to bring the person in. After the accuser and the accused made their statements, the Assembly decided whether or not to hold a trial. If the answer was yes, they sent the Scythian Archers to the Agora to round up citizens for jury duty.

The most famous Athenian trial was that of the seventy-year-old philosopher Socrates, in 399 BCE. He was charged with impiety and corrupting youth, because he had told his young followers to question everything, including the existence of the gods and the

authority of the state. Socrates went to his trial willingly, so the Scythian Archers wouldn't have had to drag him there. But it was quite likely a Scythian Archer who was Socrates's jailer, and who gave him the cup of hemlock poison to drink after he'd been found guilty and sentenced to death.

Scythian Archers even appeared as minor characters in Greek drama, though usually for comic effect. The dialogue made fun of their foreign accents. The Athenians didn't want the Scythians to forget that even though they were police, they were still slaves, and not the equals of Greeks.

ROME: URBAN COHORTS

Rome was one of the largest and most powerful cities in the ancient world. With over a million inhabitants, it became the seat of power for a vast empire. But it wasn't until after Caesar Augustus became emperor in 27 BCE that it had a police force. Augustus established the *cohortes urbanes* (urban cohorts) to bring order and security to a city that was plagued by crime. There were three cohorts in all, and each was made up of a thousand men commanded by a leader called a tribune. The tribunes answered to an official called the city prefect, who was a combination of mayor and chief of police. Augustus saw the urban cohorts as insurance against the power of the Praetorian Guard, the imperial troops who were his own bodyguards. Should the Praetorians prove disloyal, the emperor could call upon the urban cohorts.

CRIME REPORT

In 61 CE, a prefect named Lucius Secundus was murdered by one of his slaves. Roman law called for the execution of all four hundred of Secundus's slaves. An angry mob protested against the draconian measure. Emperor Nero sent the urban cohorts to disperse the crowds, and the slaves were crucified.

The men in the urban cohorts wore armor and carried spears, swords, and shields. They patrolled the streets, keeping an eye out for criminals and runaway slaves. Particular hotspots were the public baths, where thieves stole unattended clothing and other property. The urban cohorts weren't investigators, but

they would act quickly if summoned. They chased down suspects and conducted searches. In times of social strife, the urban cohorts dispersed mobs.

At night the *vigiles urbani* (urban watchmen) patrolled the streets. They were lightly armed freed slaves, commanded by tribunes who answered to the city prefect. Sleeping by day and working all night, the vigiles were a combination police and fire department. While keeping a lookout for robbers, they also watched for fires. They enforced fire regulations, and their stations throughout Rome were equipped with buckets, axes, and ladders. Because they formed bucket brigades to fight fires, the vigiles were also called *spartoli* (little bucket men).

In 64 CE, a huge fire swept through Rome. The vigiles and urban cohorts fought valiantly to contain the blaze, but it became too big too fast for their primitive equipment. The Great Fire of Rome burned for a week, destroying most of the city. Nobody knew how many people died. Slaves searched through the rubble for bodies while the urban cohorts kept the public away and guarded salvaged property from looters.

Many people believed that Emperor Nero's agents started the fire, and there were rumors that he played his lyre and sang while Rome burned. Fearful of rebellion, Nero sent the Praetorian Guard and the urban cohorts to round up anybody suspected of treason. Hundreds of people were arrested and executed. The anger against

IS THAT TOGA LEGAL?

Officials called *aediles* supervised Rome's temples, markets, and public games. They were also the toga police. Only male Roman citizens were allowed to wear the toga, and only a high-ranking Roman like a senator or magistrate could wear one with a purple hem or stripes. It was socially unacceptable for a Roman citizen to appear in public without his toga.

Nero grew. He lost the support of the army, the Praetorian Guard, and the urban cohorts. When Nero learned that the Roman senate had ordered him to be arrested and beaten to death, he committed suicide. In the power struggle that followed, the prefects of the Praetorian Guard and the vigiles were among the many who died. Being Rome's top cops was no guarantee of safety.

CHINA: FAMILY AFFAIRS AND FORENSICS

In a document written during China's Qin dynasty (221–206 BCE), a father tells an official, "I request to have the feet of my own son fettered and to have him banished to a border prefecture in Shu, with the injunction that he must not be allowed to leave the place of banishment." The unfortunate son's offense is not known, but the father's request was granted.

Law in the early Chinese empires was a mixture of government regulations and family obligations—there wasn't an official police department. A father, as head of the household, was expected to make sure everybody in the family behaved correctly. If anyone broke the rules, he could beat them or have them banished or even executed. A person convicted of a crime might not be the only one to pay for it, either. His entire extended family could be punished. Even unrelated neighbors could be caught in the net if investigators decided they had failed to report the crime. Informers were rewarded. This self-policing system enabled just a few officials to control a large population. Also, in a nation where blood feuds were common, annihilating an entire family meant that no one was left to seek revenge.

Magistrates appointed by the emperor were the principal guardians of the law. They delegated authority to officials called prefects (not to be confused with the Roman prefects), who passed it on to sub-prefects. Most prefects were influential men of high social standing, but a few were women. In their policing role, they were responsible for keeping public order and investigating crimes. However, the sub-prefects usually did most of the actual legwork. Retired soldiers served as constables.

The Chinese were probably the first to use forensics in criminal investigations. A manual written during the Qin dynasty titled *Models on Sealing and Investigation* was used to instruct prefects on how to seal off and scientifically

DEMONS PROHIBITED

Prefects in ancient China enforced strict "demon control" regulations to protect people from supernatural forces. Among other things, the regulations determined the size and shape of a house, and the number of steps in a stairway. An improperly built house might attract evil.

examine a crime scene. For a study example, it presented a case in which a body had been found hanging by a rope. The investigator had to determine if it was a case of suicide or murder.

"When investigating, it is essential carefully to examine and consider the physical traces," the manual said. It explained how the investigator should examine the rope, and take numerous measurements. He had to note if the tongue was protruding from the mouth, and whether or not the mouth emitted a sighing sound when the body was taken down and the rope removed from around the neck. Then the investigator had to remove the clothing to look for traces of blood and to see if there was any discharge of bodily wastes. There were instructions on how to question suspects, accusers, and witnesses. "In all cases of interrogating, one should first listen carefully to their words and note these down."

Later the investigator could go back to his notes and press the person being interrogated more intensely on "unexplained points." If the investigator felt that the person was lying, he could resort to the use of torture.

Trials were held in court before a magistrate. Most of those convicted were beheaded. A magistrate might spare a criminal's life, but sentence him to slavery, the loss of a limb, or forced service as a soldier in an isolated frontier garrison. Tattooing was also a form of punishment. A young man might have his face tattooed if, for example, he struck his grandfather. The tattoo marked him for life as an object of shame.

AN IMPERIAL "HEADS UP"

Any offense against the person or property of a Chinese emperor, even if unintentional, was considered a heinous crime. If a wheel fell off the emperor's chariot, the artisan who made it was executed. If you accidentally broke a gift from the emperor, you were guilty of a major insult, and you lost your head.

Kautilya (370–283 BCE), chief advisor to Emperor Chandragupta, is recognized today as the father of policing in India. He established an elaborate police system that was in effect for over a thousand years. In the cities and towns, an officer called the *nagaraka* (protector) kept order with the help of *raksinah* (constables). Armed with clubs or canes, they patrolled the streets at night. If there was serious trouble, they sent for the royal guardsmen stationed at the city gates.

In the villages, headmen and their councils had to apprehend criminals and make sure stolen property was returned to the owners. One governor required the headman of each village to take personal responsibility for any crime committed in his community or the countryside around it. If a thief or murderer was not caught, the headman was punished for the crime. That ensured that every possible effort was made to catch the criminal. It also discouraged villagers from cooperating with criminals. Rural bandits were known to pay villagers to hide and protect them.

THINK BEFORE PULLING THE CHAIN

If a subject of India's Emperor Jahangir felt he had been unfairly treated by the police or the courts, he could shake the gold-plated Chain of Justice that hung outside the palace. The emperor would listen to the person's complaint and take action if necessary. However, anyone who shook the Chain of Justice for frivolous reasons would be punished for wasting the emperor's time.

Police stations were set up along roads to reduce banditry. Duty at those stations was dangerous, because constables often had to patrol the roads between villages alone at night. The men recruited for such work sometimes weren't much different from the outlaws they were supposed to catch. According to Indian writers of the time, the police took bribes and were often drunk. Some of them abused their authority by mistreating the peasant farmers. Sometimes headmen sent petitions to the king pleading for protection from the police. The police were also unpopular because villagers suspected them of being government spies.

With India's rigid caste system, punishments for crimes depended on the social standing of both the criminal and the victim. A person

CRIME REPORT

In the 7th century CE, near the Indian town of Sakala, the Chinese scholar Hiuen Tsang and his party were attacked by bandits. A force of armed peasants called forest guards came to the rescue. They drove off the bandits and escorted the visitors to safety.

of high caste who was convicted of murder might be banished, while a person of low caste would be executed. A man found guilty of assaulting a woman of high caste could be punished with mutilation or even death, but for assaulting a woman of low caste, the man would only pay a fine. Rich people had to pay much more than poor people, simply because they could afford it.

Execution was usually by beheading. If a magistrate wanted to make an example of a criminal, he could order him to be trampled to death by elephants. It was a dramatically memorable way of sending the message that it was best not to commit criminal acts.

CHAPTER 3

LAW ENFORCEMENT IN THE MEDIEVAL WORLD

AFTER THE FALL OF THE ROMAN EMPIRE IN THE 5TH CENTURY CE, Europe and the Mediterranean world plunged into a dark, violent era called the medieval period, or the Middle Ages, which lasted nearly a thousand years. It was a time of almost constant warfare among rival kingdoms. Lawlessness was a threat to everybody's peace and security until about the 9th century, when monarchs finally began to gain control and impose their rule through a system called feudalism.

In the feudal order of the medieval world, the king was the highest legal power. He appointed powerful nobles as justices of the peace. To people of lower social rank, these nobles were "lords." They had authority to make arrests and preside over trials. However, it was necessary to dispense legal authority even further through the social ranks.

In England, every county was divided into districts called shires. Local law enforcement was the responsibility of an overseer called a reeve. In time, the shire reeve became known as the sheriff. He might be a low-ranking noble, but usually he was a commoner who had earned the trust of his lord, or who had been elected by his peers.

The sheriff had hundreds of regulations to enforce. He made sure streams were kept free of debris that could cause blockage and flooding. If an ale-wife's brew was of poor quality, or a butcher threw the cast-off parts of slaughtered animals into the street, the sheriff fined them. His deputies, armed men called bailiffs, would pay you a visit if you allowed your livestock to graze on someone else's land, if you hadn't paid your taxes, or to conscript you into military service. If a peasant farmer, who was bound by law to work on his lord's estate, ran away, the bailiffs went after him. (A peasant became legally free if he managed to hide out in a town for a year and a day.)

People went to the sheriff with a host of complaints. He settled disputes over debts. He listened to arguments about broken marriage agreements between families. If a husband accused his wife of being a scold (a nag), the sheriff sentenced the unfortunate woman to be tied to a "ducking stool" and dunked in a river or pond several times. This was meant to be a lesson to her and a warning to other wives to be submissive and obedient.

SHAME, SHAME!

Viking warriors who broke the law were expected to report it themselves and take the consequences. To have someone else report you was a matter of great shame.

The sheriff's most important responsibility was to maintain "the peace of the realm." That meant enforcing the laws against crimes like robbery and murder. Fear was considered a strong deterrent against criminal behavior, and medieval punishments were harsh. If you were to take a tour of a shire on any given day, you might see the body of a cattle thief dangling from a tall pole called a gibbet. At the gates of a castle you might see the heads of traitors impaled

on spikes. In a town or village you would likely see people who were guilty of minor offenses, such as public drunkenness or using profane language, locked in stocks or pillories—wooden instruments with holes in them that secured their arms, legs, or heads. You might even see a convicted pickpocket tied to the back of a cart and dragged through the streets from one whipping post to another. Persons convicted of witchcraft were burned at the stake.

In spite of the threat of such brutal punishments, many people became outlaws. Not all outlaws were wanted for robbery or murder, though. A person might also be on the run from the sheriff for poaching—hunting in forests that were the preserve of the king and the nobility. England's King William I had entire villages removed so the forests would be his private hunting grounds. Many displaced villagers fled deeper into the woods to live as outlaws.

Commoners often sympathized with the outlaws, which gave rise to popular tales such as those of Robin Hood. These stories ironically have a bandit for a hero, and a policeman—the Sheriff of Nottingham—for a villain.

The sheriff and his bailiffs couldn't watch everyone all the time, so the men of every community were divided into groups of at least ten, called tithings. Each member of a tithing was sworn from the age of twelve to obey the law and be loyal to the king. He was obliged to report any other member of his tithing who broke the law. Failure to do so could result in all members of the tithing being fined. This spy system had its flaws, though. Some people refused to inform on friends and relatives. Others would falsely accuse people they didn't like.

BROTHERHOOD WATCH

From the 13th century until 1835, whenever Spanish monarchs proved incapable of protecting their people from bandits and robber barons, militia-police called *hermandades* (brotherhoods) were formed. They dispensed rough justice, and became a powerful force in Spain.

When a serious crime was committed, the victim or a witness raised a hue and cry. That meant spreading an alarm throughout the community. Everybody who heard it had to immediately join in the pursuit of the fugitive.

If you were a farmer who answered the call of hue and cry, you were a legal member of a *posse comitatus*—a body of men called upon to serve the state. You had to catch the fugitive before he could reach the sanctuary of a church. There, the fugitive was believed to be under divine protection. You couldn't arrest him. You even had to provide him with food and water. Because he was in a holy place that could not be fouled, you also had to allow him to come outside so he could relieve himself. If the fugitive escaped from the church on your watch, you would be fined. Of course, angry men didn't always stick to the rules. Sometimes fugitives were starved out or tricked out.

Sanctuary in a church could not exceed forty days. After that, the fugitive had to leave and surrender all of his possessions to the coroner, an officer of the crown. Then he was banished from the kingdom.

If your party caught up to the fugitive before he could escape the territory or reach a church, his fate depended upon several circumstances. He could be legally killed if he resisted arrest, because that was considered an admission of guilt. A noble who surrendered without a fight could appeal to the king. The sheriff would take him into custody. A commoner could be executed immediately. Men were beheaded, whereas women were dragged to the nearest body of water and drowned. However, if anyone had doubts about a person's guilt, the sheriff held the prisoner for trial. A fugitive who escaped the posse was hunted down by professional "thief catchers" who were paid a bounty by the sheriff.

THE CHANGING CORONER

The duties of the coroner have changed over the centuries. Today the coroner is a government official who confirms death and investigates violent or otherwise suspicious deaths.

Some medieval noblemen were criminals who operated like modern-day gangsters. Eustace Folville of Leicestershire led one of the most notorious gangs of 14th-century England. With his brothers Laurence, Richard, Thomas, Robert, and Walter, and a band of armed thugs, Eustace committed crimes of robbery, murder, and extortion.

The Folville gang got away with their villainy for years because the eldest of the seven Folville brothers, John, was a justice of the peace and shielded them from the law. Other justices of the peace tried to prosecute them, but were bribed or threatened. However, one justice of the peace, Sir Robert Colville, couldn't be bought or intimidated. He tried to arrest the Folvilles at their stronghold in Teigh in 1330, but failed because his men were outnumbered. Nonetheless, Sir Robert was a patient officer who bided his time.

By 1338, Eustace had given up crime and bought a royal pardon. Richard was now the gang's leader. Sir Robert finally cornered him in 1340, in a dramatic clash at Teigh. When Sir Robert approached with a large company of soldiers, Richard and his men fled into the

FASHION POLICE

In 14th-century England, laws stated what clothing people could wear. Commoners could not dress like aristocrats, even if they could afford it. Furs, silks, and precious stones were strictly for nobles. If the sheriff caught you dressed "above your state," he could confiscate the clothing and accessories on the spot. If you were a lowly peasant, the belt that held up your pants had better be made of rope, and not leather.

church, expecting they would be safe under the law of sanctuary. But Sir Robert wasn't about to let the gang escape again. He ordered an attack.

The trapped outlaws shot arrows from the church windows, killing one of Sir Robert's men and wounding several others. But the attackers soon broke into the church. One by one, Richard Folville and his confederates were dragged outside and beheaded in the churchyard. Surviving documents don't name the men who were executed with Richard, but some historians believe they might have been his brothers Laurence, Thomas, Walter, and Robert.

Sir Robert Colville had put an end to a criminal gang. But he had violated the sanctity of a church. On the pope's orders, Sir

Robert and his men had to submit to public floggings. The clash between the laws of church and state could make life difficult for medieval police officers.

THE GARDENER POLICE OF THE OTTOMAN EMPIRE

When Sultan Mehmed II conquered Constantinople (now Istanbul) in 1453, he made it the capital of the vast Ottoman Empire that spread across Eastern Europe, the Middle East, and North Africa. Mehmed and his successors ruled with an iron fist from a magnificent palace complex called Yeni Saray, which was a city within a city. It had royal residences, government offices, stables, armories, and courtyards. Lovely parks and gardens graced the palace grounds.

The men who cared for the sultan's flowers and greenery were called *bastancis*. Numbering about five thousand, they were not ordinary gardeners. The bastancis were also the sultan's feared police force. They served as spies, customs inspectors, bodyguards, secret messengers, and even executioners. The bastancis' uniform was a red skullcap, muslin breeches, and

SHINING ARMOR, SMELLY KNIGHT

From the 12th to the 14th century, the Knights Templar was an unofficial police body that protected Christian pilgrims on their way to Jerusalem. These elite warriors were also monks who had taken vows of chastity, and were forbidden to bathe—ever!

an open shirt that revealed their muscular chests and arms.

The bastancis enforced the rules concerning all state and ceremonial proceedings. Those rules defined the duties of government officials, and even dictated what clothes they could wear and the lengths of their beards. One of the bastancis' most sinister duties was enforcing Mehmed II's "law of fratricide."

Mehmed believed that when a sultan died, the throne should pass not to his eldest son, but to the strongest male member of the family. The first one to seize power had the right to eliminate every relative who might challenge his claim. The most ruthless would-be successor would send the bastancis to murder his own brothers and his other male kin. Because sultans had numerous wives, the bastancis could have a lot of royal relatives to dispose of. When Mehmed III ascended to the Ottoman throne in 1595, his victims included nineteen siblings. The method of execution for royalty was strangulation with a silken cord.

Not all new sultans had every male relative killed. Some would have their inconvenient kin imprisoned in suites of rooms deep within the palace complex, where they lived in comfort. Bastancis kept close watch on them. The only way a prisoner could get out

CRIME REPORT

The bastancis themselves could suffer the sultan's wrath. Mehmed II had several executed when a prized cucumber was stolen from his vegetable garden.

of the "gilded cage" was if the sultan sent for him, and that might never happen.

If you were a government minister or a general, you dreaded a visit from the bastancis, because that meant you had displeased the sultan. They took you before the sultan, and you would be allowed a formal hearing. Then you would be given a cup of sherbet. White sherbet meant that your life was spared. Red sherbet meant death. But because you were an important person, you wouldn't have to endure the indignity of dying in front of a common crowd. You would be executed with a silken cord in the privacy of an inner court.

If you were a man of the highest rank, the sultan might give you a chance to save your own life. You and the bastanci executioner would run a three-hundred-yard race. If you won, your death sentence was commuted to banishment. If you lost, the bastanci was waiting with the silken cord.

Just inside the palace's main gate was the Fountain of the Executioner. The bastancis dragged common criminals there to be publicly beheaded with swords. After the day's executions, the bastancis washed the blood off their hands in the fountain. The heads of thieves, murderers, and traitors were impaled on spikes above the palace gates. Condemned women weren't executed with the silken cord or the sword. The bastancis sewed them up alive in sacks weighted with heavy stones and dropped them into the sea.

The bastancis were never more feared than they were during the time of Sultan Selim I, who was known as "the Grim." During his short reign, from 1512 to 1520, more than thirty thousand people were executed. He made the Fountain of the Executioner the most dreaded and hated symbol of the sultans' power over life and death.

Three centuries later, in 1845, efforts were made to modernize the Ottoman government. Administrators established a regular police force based on the Western European model. The new police were controlled by a city council, not a temperamental sultan. The bastancis went back to gardening.

JAPAN: SWORDS OF THE SAMURAI

Japan's medieval period was an age of warriors. All Japanese people looked upon the emperor as divine, but he was usually a figurehead with little actual political power. The real rulers were warlords called *shoguns*. By the late 12th century, Japan was divided into many small regions governed by *daimyo* (great lords), who each owed allegiance to a shogun. The shoguns and daimyo made up their own rules and regulations. For law enforcement, they had samurai warriors. The samurai were highly skilled in the use of weapons—especially the famous samurai sword, which only they could own. When the samurai weren't fighting their masters' wars with rival shoguns and

ODOR IN THE COURT

Ooka Tadasuke, a samurai, was chief of police and magistrate in 18th-century Edo. Once, an innkeeper brought a student into court, complaining that the student had stolen the wonderful aroma of some food he'd been cooking. Tadasuke told the student to pass some coins from one hand to the other. Then he told the innkeeper that the sound of the coins was payment for the smell of the food.

daimyo, or suppressing peasant revolts, they served in other capacities, often acting as local administrators or police.

Crime against property was much less of a problem in Japan than it was in Europe. That was due to a system of "enforced stability." Strict regulations touched every aspect of daily life. They told you what clothes you could wear, what foods you could eat, what work you could do, and where you could live. They even dictated where you could build a toilet. Unauthorized travel outside your community was forbidden. Outdoor activity at night was restricted. The many regulations kept people in their place; they also kept the crime rate low.

In cities like Edo (now Tokyo), the samurai kept the streets orderly and free of thieves, and enforced fire laws. In the villages, headmen punished petty offenders with fines and forced labor. A particularly troublesome person could be banished. The headman had to report serious crimes to his shogun or daimyo. It was in a headman's best interest to make sure the people in his community were law-abiding, because a whole family or even an entire village could be punished for one person's wrongdoing.

Sometimes bandits roamed the countryside, raiding villages and robbing travelers. Usually they were criminals who had been expelled from the cities or peasants who had been banished from their villages. Samurai would make short work of bandit gangs. They beheaded captured bandits just to test the sharpness of their swords.

However, a person didn't have to be a robber to suffer swift decapitation by a samurai. A samurai could behead any lower-class person, on the spot, for anything that could be taken as "rude behavior." If a peasant didn't kneel down quickly enough and bow low enough when a shogun rode by, for example, he could lose his head. Being out after dark without permission, speaking disrespectfully to a daimyo or samurai, or even giving a person an inappropriate present were among the many "crimes" against acceptable behavior that were punishable by death. Samurai who were found guilty of breaking the law took their own lives in a ritual suicide called *seppuku*.

CHAPTER 4

THE BIRTH OF POLICE DEPARTMENTS

THE MODERN CONCEPT OF POLICE EVOLVED IN THE CITIES OF Western Europe. The period from the 14th century to the 16th century was one of great change. The Middle Ages gave way to the Renaissance, a period spanning roughly three hundred years that saw dramatic advances in the arts, sciences, and in social philosophies. Exploration and improvements in navigation opened up a much wider world to seafaring European nations. Because of increased trade, villages became towns, and towns became cities.

Many people moved to towns and cities to work at a multitude of trades and services. But not everybody was looking for an honest job. Vagabonds and outlaws who had once hidden in the forests found that they could lose themselves in the crowded, bustling urban centers. Between wars, soldiers who had been discharged from the army poured into the towns. If they couldn't find employment, they turned to robbery.

As always, poverty spawned crime. Men, women, and children who had no money and no work stole so they could eat. The old rural methods of law enforcement were not effective in towns, especially at night when ruffians and thieves prowled the dark streets. One of the earliest forms of new urban policing was called the Watch.

If you lived in a town in Elizabethan England (Queen Elizabeth I reigned from 1558 to 1603), the local high constable called on you from time to time to take your turn on the Watch. It was an unpaid duty you performed as a loyal subject of the queen. If you refused, you could be fined or put in jail.

The Watch patrolled the streets after curfew. That word comes from the French *couvre-feu*, which means "cover fire." Since most of the buildings in towns were made of wood, fire was a constant danger. At a specified time, usually eight p.m., everyone had to "bank" the fires in their homes. They covered a bed of hot coals with a layer of ash or cinders that kept the fire alive, but low.

As a member of the Watch, you walked through the streets, ringing a bell to let people know it was curfew. You peeked in windows to make sure nobody had gone to bed and left a fire blazing. If anyone did, you'd pound on the door until somebody got up and banked it.

There were no streetlights, so the streets and alleys you patrolled were dark. In some towns, householders were required to leave a lamp burning outside the

BLADE CONTROL

England's Queen Elizabeth I issued a law that limited the length of daggers to 30 centimeters (12 inches), and swords to 91 centimeters (36 inches). Anyone caught with an illegal blade had it confiscated and broken on the spot. Persons making or selling them were prosecuted.

The queen declared that such blades were not made for self-defense, but for murder, and were therefore a threat to the peace of the realm.

front door. You would carry a lantern to light your way through the darkest places, and to help you avoid stepping in puddles, garbage, and horse droppings.

You also watched for people who were on the streets after curfew. Honest working people went to bed early, so anyone who was outside at night was suspected of being up to no good. You would be on the lookout for "draw-latches" (burglars) and "footpads" (muggers).

The penalty for robbery was death, so thieves ran for their lives if they were detected by the Watch. Your job was to catch and arrest them. You would call for help from other members of the Watch and from local residents. When you caught a culprit, he'd be taken to the nearest Watchhouse to be locked up until the court took custody of him. You carried a long, stout staff as a weapon in case a suspect resisted arrest.

SORRY, I'M SICK TODAY

King Fernando I founded Portugal's first police force in 1383. Called *quadrilheiros*, they were conscripted from among Lisbon's strongest men. They patrolled the streets and apprehended criminals, but were not paid. It was dangerous work, and injuries were frequent. Men often tried to find a way to escape the duty.

Sometimes you'd come upon a curfew-breaker who wasn't a criminal. If that person was an aristocrat, you'd let him go on his way as long as he wasn't behaving in a disorderly manner. If he was a commoner, he'd have to go with you to the Watchhouse and explain to a constable why he was in violation of the curfew.

The Watch was called upon for certain daytime duties, too. Marketplaces and fairs were prime hunting grounds for pickpockets and "cut-purses," experts at swiftly and quietly cutting the strings that tied a man's purse to his belt. You'd have to be sharp-eyed to spot such crafty robbers in a crowded place.

Another of your duties at fairs and markets was keeping the public peace. If a fight started, you would break it up and take the offending parties to a constable. You'd also be on the lookout for weapons. Swords, daggers, and firearms were forbidden at fairs and in marketplaces.

By carrying out your Watch duties, you contributed to the safety and security of your town. You showed you were a responsible member of your community. In recognition of this, on special holidays you were allowed the honor of marching in parades along with town officials and the local aristocracy.

PARIS: SWAGGERING BAILIFFS TO CITY OF LIGHTS

Renaissance Paris was a crime-ridden town, plagued by cut-purses, burglars, and "wool-snatchers"—thieves who grabbed expensive cloaks from people's shoulders and ran off with them. The first Paris police were bailiffs who were an extension of the royal bodyguard. They were concerned more with ferreting out suspected traitors than with catching thieves and murderers. The bailiffs themselves were often a threat to the public peace, swaggering around armed with swords, helping themselves to food and drink, and bullying residents. Parisians called them *ribauds*, the name given to soldiers who behaved like bandits.

The office of the provost marshal, established in the 12th century, wasn't much of an improvement. The king usually appointed a non-native of Paris to this post, because he thought an outsider would have no connections with the city's criminal gangs. Nonetheless, so many provost marshals were corrupt that Parisians called them "kings of the ribauds." By the 17th century, the crime rate in Paris was so bad that one observer wrote, "Assassinations, armed robberies, debaucheries and all forms of excess reign supreme."

In 1665 the senior police official of Paris was murdered. A royal committee advised King Louis XIV to establish a new form of policing for the city. The king inaugurated the office of the Lieutenant General of Paris in 1667. He gave its first command to a former magistrate named Nicolas de la Reynie. This was the beginning of the world's first modern, urban police department.

De la Reynie had advanced views on law enforcement. "Policing," he wrote, "consists of ensuring the safety of the public and of private individuals, by protecting the city from that which causes disorder." He completely reorganized the chaotic system of law enforcement in Paris, starting by merging four rival "police" departments into one. He increased the number of inspectors, and made them police chiefs in the city's seventeen districts. They had to report to him daily.

To back up his constables, de la Reynie was authorized to call on the royal troops who were stationed in Paris. He also developed a network of paid spies who kept him informed of what was happening in Paris's underworld. He called his spies in the streets "flies," and those in the prisons "sheep." With such strength behind him, and skillful organization, de la Reynie crushed the criminal gangs that infested the city.

CRIME REPORT

One of de la Reynie's most famous cases was the Affair of the Poisons. Between 1677 and 1682, a series of mysterious deaths alarmed the French aristocracy, including King Louis XIV, who feared assassination by poison. Stories circulated about deadly potions, witchcraft, and devil worship. De la Reynie rounded up dozens of suspects, who gave up more names under torture. His investigations resulted in the executions of thirty-six people.

De la Reynie went beyond making the city uncomfortable for criminals. He arranged for beggars to be given aid instead of punishment. He set up a program for the rescue and care of abandoned infants. He cracked down on dueling, to the anger of aristocrats who believed it was their right to settle differences with swords or pistols. And he banned men of all classes from taking weapons into the theaters.

Traffic and parking regulations were just a few of the many other new ideas de la Reynie brought to policing in Paris. And de la Reynie was largely responsible for the introduction of the street lamps that gave Paris the name "the City of Lights." Constables arrested anybody they caught vandalizing the lamps.

De la Reynie was the lieutenant governor of the Paris police for thirty years. He made enemies, of course, because not everybody liked his methods. But he left behind a safer Paris, and a police department that became a model for other European cities.

AMSTERDAM: NEIGHBORHOOD WATCH

Amsterdam, the capital of the Dutch Republic, was a major seaport and one of the most important trading centers in Europe. The city was famous for its canals, but there was something else that made Amsterdam unique among the great cities of Western Europe.

If you were a foreigner visiting Amsterdam around 1650, you would find that the busy streets were free of beggars, drunks, and rowdies. Men walked around unarmed. Women left their homes to go to the market unaccompanied by men. If you spoke to local

residents, you'd learn that people didn't even lock their doors when they went out.

Of course, there *were* criminals in Amsterdam, and throughout the Dutch Republic. But the Dutch had developed a system of maintaining law and order that made their communities among the safest in Europe. The low crime rates resulted from cooperation between citizens and police.

Thriving commerce brought prosperity to Amsterdam during the 17th century. But the city was not completely free of poverty. To prevent crime, the municipal government provided assistance for people who qualified as "deserving poor." These were Amsterdam

residents who couldn't work for a living because of illness, injury, or old age. Guards at the city gates kept out non-resident vagrants and vagabonds.

The rules for the "deserving poor" were strict. If you committed a crime, you lost your eligibility. You also had to attend church on Sunday. You would be disqualified if you were caught gambling or if you were seen entering a tavern.

The *almoner*, the official in charge of poor relief, would know if and when a person broke the rules, because every neighborhood had a "Watch" made up of local citizens and led by an elected *burgher* (a prominent member of the community). These men were paid to patrol the streets at night. If they caught a suspected criminal, they took him to a neighborhood jail where he'd be held for the *schout* (sheriff) or one of his deputies. In the event of a serious disturbance, the burgher could send for the civic militia, men who served as part-time citizen-soldiers.

The Watch not only prevented crime and apprehended lawbreakers, it also upheld a code of decency. Public drunkenness was frowned upon. Wife-beating and abusive treatment of servants was unacceptable. Such behavior was reported to the schout and could result in embarrassment for the offender when it was announced in church on Sunday. Amsterdam's neighborhood watch system was so successful that the city's schout was able to maintain a high level of law and order with the assistance of only a few deputies.

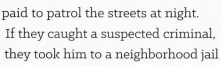

LIGHT! THE POLICE OFFICER'S FRIEND

The 17th century Dutch artist and inventor Jan van der Heyden designed a glass and metal streetlamp that let out the flame's smoke, but could not be extinguished by wind. More than eighteen hundred of the new lamps were distributed throughout Amsterdam. Good lighting at night discouraged crime, and decreased the incidence of people accidentally falling into the canals and drowning.

THE SOLDIER POLICE OF MOSCOW

Peter the Great, czar of Russia from 1682 to 1725, admired Western European ways. He felt that the Russians lagged behind the French, English, and Dutch in such things as science, education, the arts, and social development. The Russians stubbornly clung to old medieval ways, but Peter was determined to drag his country into the modern world—whether his people liked it or not. Among those who resisted Peter's new changes were Moscow's police, the *streltsy*, who had been on duty since the mid-16th century.

The streltsy were Russian soldiers. The name meant "shooters," because they were armed with muskets. They wore long coats of blue, green, or red, with matching fur-lined hats. Their breeches (pants) were tucked into yellow boots with turned-up toes. Swords hung from their black leather belts. Every streltsy soldier had a full, thick beard, which was a mark of masculinity in Russia.

The streltsy lived in their own neighborhoods in Moscow. The government provided them with homes, clothing, and food. Because they weren't paid very much money, they were allowed to operate businesses. They were also exempt from taxes. Some of them became rich.

The streltsy guarded Moscow's city gates and the Kremlin, the center of political power in Russia. They escorted the czar wherever he went. If a fire broke out, the streltsy rushed to fight it. Streltsy armed with small, knotted whips called *knouts* patrolled Moscow's streets. They apprehended criminals and broke up the drunken brawls for which Moscow was notorious. Most people tried to keep out of their way.

The streltsy had gained enough wealth and influence by the late 17th century to wield considerable power in Moscow. They held very conservative views, and didn't like the "foreign" changes Czar Peter was bringing to Russia. Among other things—such as a ban on the old practice of arranged marriages, and improvements in the status of women—Peter decreed that Russian men had to shave off their beards, which he thought made them look uncivilized.

In 1698 the streltsy rebelled, hoping to replace Peter with his sister Sophia. Peter crushed the revolt ruthlessly. Over the next few years, more than a thousand streltsy were tortured and executed. Many more, mostly younger men, were branded and sent into exile. Streltsy units that had not participated in the rebellion were disbanded.

In Moscow, soldiers of the elite Preobrazhensky Regiment, which had been formed by the czar himself, took over policing duties. In 1702 a new police organization called the Secret Office was formally instituted. Its principal purpose was to root out traitors. The Secret Office was effective in that task, but Russia remained far behind the developments in policing that were happening elsewhere.

THE BOW STREET RUNNERS: LONDON'S FIRST PROFESSIONAL POLICE

By the early 18th century, London had become a sprawling metropolis and was the largest city in Europe. It was also the capital of the still-expanding British Empire. But in spite of London's wealth, many of its inhabitants were poor. Thieves and thugs prowled its streets and alleys, and the crime rate was high.

In 1749, Henry Fielding, a famous author, was appointed magistrate. His court was at 4 Bow Street. He founded a new police force that became known as the Bow Street Runners—a name the constables didn't like because "runner" was considered a derogatory term. They were paid a small amount of money by the government, making them London's first "professional" police officers, but depended mostly on rewards paid by private citizens and businesses for financial support. They didn't wear uniforms until 1805.

Fielding started with just six constables. They didn't patrol the streets, but were sent out to serve writs and apprehend criminals. They had the authority to make arrests anywhere in Britain. Because they tracked down wanted fugitives, the Bow Street Runners were England's first police detectives. Some of them, like

John Townsend, became famous. He even served as a bodyguard for King George III.

Henry Fielding retired in 1754, and was succeeded by John Fielding, his blind half-brother. John became known as the Blind Beak of Bow Street. In spite of his handicap, he was a remarkable officer who learned to recognize the voices of more than three thousand criminals, and founded the popular magazine that would become *The Police Gazette*. In 1763 John Fielding added the Bow Street Horse Patrol to the police services. These mounted constables patrolled the roads outside London, protecting travelers from robbers called highwaymen. He was also instrumental in bringing streetlights to London.

The Bow Street Runners were an important step forward in policing, but crime remained a major problem in London and other large British cities. Then, late in the 18th century, a Scottish magistrate named Patrick Colquhoun became one of the first officials to approach policing as a science. He wrote that police duties should include detection of crime, the apprehension of offenders, and the prevention of crime through a presence of police in the public. He also said that a well-regulated police force should be a separate unit within the government, with a series of checks and balances to limit its political power. Colquhoun's ideas inspired many civic leaders, including the man who became known as the father of modern policing.

CRIME REPORT

Jerry Abershaw, a notorious 18th-century highwayman, was hanged for shooting two Bow Street Runners, killing one and wounding the other.

SIR ROBERT PEEL AND THE BOBBIES

On September 29, 1829, a new figure in law enforcement appeared on the streets of London. He wore a long-tailed blue coat and a top hat. In a big pocket he carried a wooden club called a truncheon, a pair of handcuffs, and a wooden rattle he could use to summon help. He was part of a thousand-man force instituted by Home Secretary Sir Robert Peel to fight crime in England's largest city.

The "Peelers," as they were originally called, belonged to the Metropolitan London Police Department, the city's first official policing institution. They were a uniformed force created by parliamentary legislation called the Metropolitan Police Act, and paid only by the government. They would eventually be called "bobbies." The top hat was replaced by a distinctive helmet, and a shrill whistle proved more effective than the rattle. But the truncheon remained the bobby's principal weapon well into modern times. It became a point of pride that the bobby didn't need a firearm to enforce law and order.

To be a constable on Sir Robert Peel's police force you had to be strong and tough. Your pay was little more than that of a common laborer. You worked seven days a week, with only five unpaid holidays in the whole year. You couldn't get married without permission. You had to wear your uniform even when you were off-duty.

As a bobby in Victorian London (Queen Victoria reigned from 1837 to 1901), you were a figure of respect. Most people saw you not only as a symbol of authority, but also as a friend. You might be called upon to settle a family dispute or an argument between a shopkeeper and a customer. In the event of an accident or illness, people would call on you for help. This was something

BOBBIES! WHAT ABOUT THE CHARLIES?

In the 17th century, England's King Charles II established a group of royal watchmen who were called "Charlies," after him. They weren't very good policemen, preferring drinking and gambling in the taverns to patrolling the dark streets.

new. Previously, police had been seen only as the strong arm of the law, and the general public wanted as little to do with them as possible. As a bobby, you were a pioneer: the first helpful cop walking a beat (the route a constable follows on foot patrol).

But there were others who would quickly duck out of sight if they saw you coming. These were the denizens of London's underworld—the thieves and other criminals you would know as well as you did the respectable people. It was important that you knew who those people were, what they were up to, and who might have useful information. This was also new to policing: constables who were on the streets, watching and listening, trying to be in touch with everything that went on in the neighborhood.

YOU COULD SET YOUR WATCH BY HIM

Few residents of London's shabby working-class districts owned timepieces. They kept track of time by factory whistles, church bells, and the opening and closing of shops. At night, they might even mark the hour by the sound of the footsteps of a passing bobby walking his beat.

You weren't a government spy in disguise, but a visible representative of law and order, working for the good of the community.

Your job could be dangerous, especially at night. Parts of the sprawling city were poorly lit. Blankets of fog often enveloped London, making the light of the gas lamps feeble in the mist. You walked your patrol alone, never knowing what might be waiting around the next corner. But you were confident in knowing that if you encountered trouble, a blast on your whistle would bring other bobbies, who were walking their beats just blocks away.

SCOTLAND YARD

At first, the Metropolitan London Police Department was reluctant to have any of its constables work as plainclothes detectives, out of concern that the public would view them as government secret police. For years only one detective, a former member of the Bow Street Runners, worked for the police. Then in 1842, a particularly difficult murder case made obvious the need for specialized criminal investigators.

The new "Detective Force" started with just eight men. Their duties included watching the activities of known criminals in London's vast underworld, investigating certain murder cases, and listening for any threats against Parliament or the royal family. The original Metropolitan Police headquarters was in a building called Whitehall Place that backed onto a street named Old Scotland Yard. The origin of the street name is lost in legend, but "Scotland Yard" eventually replaced the term Detective Force.

Scotland Yard became famous for solving murders, robberies, and other serious crimes. Its methods were adopted by police departments in other countries. One of its most significant accomplishments was establishing the importance of detective work in preventing crime. An example was the "dead letter" case of 1876, which became one of the most sensational crime stories of the time.

An unclaimed letter addressed to "M.Q." via general delivery at a suburban London post office wound up in the dead letter department (where unclaimed mail was stored). A clerk opened and read the letter. It appeared that the author, who signed the letter "W.K.V.," was planning to poison someone. The post office turned the letter over to Scotland Yard. Inspector George Clark was put on the case.

WHAT'S IN A NAME?

Today, the Metropolitan London Police Service is commonly known as the Met. In the colorful slang of the Cockney section of London, the police department is called the "Old Bill." The term Scotland Yard was never an official name for the police, but when the Met moved into a new, modern building in 1967, the headquarters was officially called New Scotland Yard.

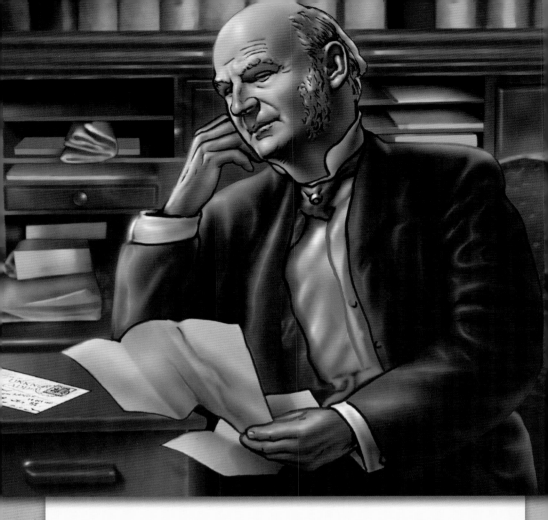

Clark found enough clues in the letter to trace it to the author, Dr. William Kingston Vance. Further investigation revealed that the mysterious "M.Q." stood for Mister Quarll, a false name. The person's real name was Ellen Snee.

Because of health problems, Ellen wanted to take her own life. At that time suicide was called "self-murder," and it caused serious social and legal problems for surviving family members. Ellen had paid Dr. Vance to provide her with a poison that he claimed would make her death appear to have been natural.

Inspector Clark intervened before Ellen Snee could kill herself. Dr. Vance was arrested, tried, and sent to prison for conspiracy to commit murder. It was a very unusual case because the "victim" desired her own death, but it demonstrated the value of good detective skills.

However, criminal investigation techniques were still at an early stage, and not very sophisticated. That became clear in 1881 with a series of horrific murders committed by a killer known as Jack the Ripper. Scotland Yard put its best detectives on the case, and every bobby in London watched for any sign of a suspect. But the Ripper was never caught.

Investigators of that time relied heavily on witnesses to help them solve crimes, and nobody had seen or heard anything that might put the police on the Ripper's trail. Bobbies, who were usually the first police officers to reach a crime scene, sometimes unintentionally ruined evidence before detectives arrived. Morgue attendants undressed and washed the body of one of the Ripper's victims, destroying possible clues before a police

DICKENS AND DOYLE

Novelist Charles Dickens was a good friend of Scotland Yard inspector Charles Frederick Field, and once wrote an essay about him titled "On Duty With Inspector Field." Dickens used Field as the model for the character Inspector Bucket in his 1852 novel *Bleak House*. Sir Arthur Conan Doyle was another author who found inspiration in Scotland Yard. However, the Scotland Yard investigators in Doyle's stories are never as clever as his greatest literary creation, the master detective Sherlock Holmes.

CRIME REPORT

Dr. Thomas Bond studied autopsy reports on Jack the Ripper's victims, and wrote a report on what he thought were the killer's physical, mental, and psychological characteristics. This report, written in November 1888, is the first documented example of criminal profiling.

doctor could examine it. Most significantly, the police had never before dealt with the type of homicidal maniac identified today as a serial killer. The landmark case made clear the need for improved methods of criminal investigation.

CHAPTER 5

FROM THE OLD WEST TO DOWN UNDER

POLICING IN WHAT ARE NOW CANADA, THE UNITED STATES, and Australia was largely based on the British model. These countries were all British colonies at one time. Even though the United States broke away from the British Empire in the American Revolution (1775–83), it still retained many British ideas and traditions concerning law and justice.

During North America's colonial period, communities in Canada and the U.S. had sheriffs. In the 19th century, local governments in the two countries established police departments very much like the one in London. Constables in cities like New York and Toronto even wore bobby-style uniforms and helmets.

But as settlement moved west across the North American frontier, people had to adapt to isolation and rugged conditions. Some towns in the American West were "wide open," lacking any form of official government, including police. Such towns became the haunts of outlaws, and were notorious for violence. To combat lawlessness, local citizens would elect or hire a sheriff or marshal. His symbol of office was a badge.

THE WILD WEST:
THE MAN WITH THE BADGE

In the movies, lawmen of the American West are heroes who shoot it out with desperadoes. In real life, the man with the badge was a police officer who carried out many duties. As sheriff or marshal, he had to be a reliable, responsible member of the community. He collected taxes, issued licenses, served court orders, and stopped people from racing horses and buggies in the streets. He enforced sanitation and fire regulations, fined dishonest shopkeepers, and collared boys playing hooky from school. The lawman's job was more likely to involve paperwork than gunfights. Many frontier towns were peaceful places where shoot-outs never happened.

But the booming cowtowns and mining towns could be wild and woolly places. Tough cowboys and miners would drink, gamble, and brawl. Sometimes they galloped their horses up and down the main street, whooping and firing their guns in the air—which was dangerous, because the bullets had to come down somewhere.

Legendary gunfighters like Marshal Wild Bill Hickok became famous for "taming" rough towns like Abilene and Dodge City. The cowboys who drove large herds of cattle north from Texas to these Kansas railroad towns liked to raise hell in the saloons and on the streets. However, if the town had a tough, fast-shooting lawman, they wanted no trouble with him.

WANTED:
SPOT AND ROVER

Wild Bill Hickok, the famous marshal of Abilene, Kansas, was paid a twenty-five-cent bounty for every stray dog he shot.

LYNCH LAW

Vigilantes are citizens who illegally take the law into their own hands. In the Wild West era there were many instances in which alleged criminals were lynched (hanged) without a fair trial. One such victim was Ellen "Cattle Kate" Watson of Wyoming, suspected of being a rustler.

Most western communities had bylaws against carrying guns within town limits. That was important not only for the peace and quiet of the community and the safety of the residents, but also for the protection of the lawmen themselves. One of the most dangerous jobs for a lawman was disarming drunks.

The most famous gun battle in the history of the Wild West was triggered in Tombstone, Arizona, when some men broke the law against carrying guns in town. Virgil Earp was the marshal, and his brothers Wyatt and Morgan were his deputies. Tombstone's most notorious troublemakers were the Clanton and McLaury brothers, suspected cattle rustlers and stagecoach robbers.

On October 26, 1881, the Clanton-McLaury gang was at the OK Corral, armed and making threats against the Earps. Backed by Wyatt, Morgan, and a gunman named Doc Holliday, Virgil demanded that the gang hand over their guns. The shoot-out that followed lasted less than a minute. Three members of the Clanton-McLaury gang were killed.

LONE STAR LAW

Established in 1823, the Texas Rangers are the oldest state law enforcement body in the United States. They became famous for chasing down outlaws. A Texas Ranger named Frank Hamer led the posse that killed the notorious bandits Bonnie and Clyde in 1934.

The showdown at the OK Corral became romanticized in fiction. Wyatt Earp emerged from the stories as a heroic figure who was everything people thought a lawman should be: courageous and fast on the draw. However, such violent incidents brought about a mythical image of what policing in the Old West was really like. The quietly efficient man with the badge who kept his town safe without dramatic gunfights just didn't fit into the popular legends of the Wild West.

CRIME REPORT

The violence didn't end at the OK Corral. Soon after the famous gun battle, a hidden assassin killed Morgan Earp, and an ambush left Virgil with a crippled arm. Wyatt Earp and Doc Holliday tracked down and killed the men they believed were responsible for the attacks.

THE NORTH WEST MOUNTED POLICE: CANADA'S SCARLET RIDERS

In 1869 the young Dominion of Canada acquired from the Hudson's Bay Company the vast western territory called Rupert's Land. It stretched from present-day Manitoba all the way to the Rocky Mountains, and included what are now the provinces of Saskatchewan and Alberta. It was wild, sparsely populated country, home to diverse Native peoples, including the Métis, and a few white trappers and traders.

The Canadian government founded the North West Mounted Police (NWMP) in 1873 to deal with a major problem in the West. American traders had set up illegal whiskey posts from which they sold a hellish brew of raw alcohol mixed with gunpowder, tobacco juice, red ink, and other vile additives. The most notorious post was Fort Whoop-Up, but there were many others scattered across the prairies and in the foothills of the Rockies. The whiskey posts became centers of drunken violence, and the whiskey trade had a devastating effect on the Native population.

Prime Minister John A. Macdonald had another strong motive for sending a police force west. In the United States there had been talk of annexing the fertile prairies to the north. The presence of Canadian police would help establish Canada's sovereignty.

The NWMP spent a year recruiting men. The hard training and strict discipline weeded out all but the best. Besides being of "good moral character," recruits had to be good horsemen, because they would spend a lot of time in the saddle. The men also had to be tough and dedicated, because they were in for a brutal journey before they even faced the outlaw whiskey traders.

The march to the West that the first NWMP constables and officers made in 1874 became a Canadian epic of endurance and determination. The constables looked impressive in their scarlet tunics, but they were new to the rugged conditions of the West. There were no roads, the weather was terrible, clouds of mosquitoes and blackflies tormented them, food ran low, and there were long stretches between sources of good drinking water. Many horses

died along the way. Had it not been for the assistance of a resourceful Métis guide named Jerry Potts, the expedition might have failed.

The police expected to meet stiff resistance from the American whiskey traders—some of whom were notorious gunmen. The traders in Fort Whoop-Up were even equipped with cannons. But to the officers' surprise, the whiskey men fled without a fight. The outlaws had no desire to shoot it out with the Mounties. The NWMP had rid the Canadian West of a major criminal element without firing a shot. The Mounties went on to earn a reputation for courage and efficiency as they hunted down lawbreakers. Mounties rescued people trapped by blizzards, or those who were sick or injured. They found lost children, as well as wandering livestock thought to have been stolen. For many a farmer, rancher, or trapper living in an isolated location, the Mountie on patrol was a welcome visitor. When a gold rush drew thousands of adventurers to Canada's Yukon Territory in the late 1890s, the Mounties were sent north to keep law and order. Due to their presence, the Yukon had little of the lawlessness that plagued gold rushes in California and Alaska.

As national police, NWMP constables had broader authority than American lawmen did in their country. The many "Indian wars" that erupted in the American West weren't repeated in the Canadian West. The Mounties worked to establish a good relationship with Native leaders while also enforcing treaties on behalf of the federal government.

The Mounties were instrumental in setting the stage for settlement of the West by immigrant ranchers and farmers, which forever changed the lifestyle of Native peoples. The NWMP eventually became the Royal Canadian Mounted Police, a force that continues to operate in many parts of Canada today.

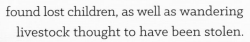

MISTAKEN MOTTO

There has long been an incorrect belief that the Mounties' motto is "We always get our man." That came from an article in the Fort Benton, Montana, *Record* in 1877, which said, "The M.P.s (Mounted Police) are worse than bloodhounds when they scent the track of a smuggler, and they fetch their men everytime." The actual motto is *"Maintiens le Droit"* (Maintain the Law).

AUSTRALIA: POLICING DOWN UNDER

Australia became a British colony in 1770. It was a continent of vast unexplored territories, sparsely populated by the native Aborigines. Because Australia was so far away, few British people wanted to go there to live. The British government came up with a plan that solved two problems. Instead of putting convicted criminals into already overcrowded prisons, the authorities would pack them into the holds of ships and send them to Australia.

A number of the crimes were of a very minor nature--such as stealing a hairbrush--and some of the prisoners were as young as nine, though they also included thieves from the streets of London and rebels from Ireland. They labored in prisons called penal colonies under brutal conditions. Most of them remained in Australia when their sentences expired.

Freed convicts could look for employment in a town like Sydney, the principal settlement, or they could hire themselves out to farmers and ranchers. Some ex-convicts obtained their own land and became successful at raising crops and livestock. However, many fled into the wild Australian countryside and became bushrangers.

The bushrangers were outlaws who lived by armed robbery and rustling livestock. They sold sheep, cattle, horses, and other stolen property at low prices to settlers in outlying areas. To struggling farmers and ranchers, the bushrangers were Robin Hoods. The British governor, Sir Thomas Brisbane, didn't agree.

The small police department in Sydney wasn't equipped to chase bushrangers. So in 1825, Brisbane founded a mounted police force whose principal task was to hunt the outlaws down. The constables wore uniforms similar to those of the British army, and broad-brimmed hats. They were armed with swords, pistols, and batons (clubs). However, for riding in rough country the police often exchanged their uniforms for "bush clothes" and left the swords behind.

The mounted police operated out of posts called outstations. Each constable was responsible for the care of his horse, and those who neglected their mounts were severely disciplined. In Australia's desert region, some constables rode camels. On long patrols through remote regions, mounted police explored much of Australia's uncharted wilderness.

Although the mounted police represented law and order, they weren't popular with everyone. Ex-convicts who earned honest livings complained of police harassment. Even free settlers received unwelcome visits from police who suspected them of aiding bush-rangers. The result was a longstanding feeling of resentment toward police and government authority.

Nonetheless, there were numerous incidents of police heroism in the decades-long conflict with the bushrangers. Many constables died in the line of duty in gun battles with the outlaws. The clash between the police and the gang led by Ned Kelly, the most notorious of all the bushrangers, became as famous in Australian history as the shoot-out at the OK Corral was in American history. But it wasn't the most significant confrontation involving Australian police.

In 1851, a gold rush in Australia drew thousands of fortune hunters. Many police constables quit the force to dig for gold. To make up for the manpower shortage, the colonial government enlisted ex-convicts as police—with dramatic consequences.

Ex-convict policemen extorted gold from the diggers, as the miners were called. Some constables were also involved in "sly-grogging," the illegal sale of alcohol. But the biggest digger complaint concerned the license fees they had to pay for the right to dig for gold. Police frequently visited the camps, looking for anyone whose license fee wasn't paid up. The diggers protested that they had no representation in the government that taxed them through those fees. A series of violent incidents, including a bank robbery, a murder, and a disastrous fire—all of which went unsolved—led to a climactic confrontation.

PROTECTORS?

Under the 1909 New South Wales Aborigines Protection Act, police functions extended to determining who received rations, removing children to "training homes," and determining whether an Aborigine was sufficiently ill to warrant a doctor's visit.

On December 3, 1854, a combined force of police and soldiers clashed with the diggers in the Battle of the Eureka Stockade. The poorly armed diggers were quickly defeated. However, the troubles in the gold fields revealed serious problems with the colonial administration, and led to political reforms and a complete restructuring of the Australian national police. The Battle of the Eureka Stockade is regarded today as Australia's first important step toward democracy. And as for the police, the modern Mounted Section is a small, elite unit of the New South Wales Police Force.

CHAPTER 6

THE 20TH CENTURY

ON JANUARY 1, 1900, PEOPLE AWOKE TO AN UNUSUAL NEW YEAR'S Day. It was the first day of the 20th century. The world was in the midst of great change. Things like railroads, steam-powered machinery, and electric lighting hadn't existed a hundred years earlier. Inventors like Thomas Edison and Alexander Graham Bell, already famous for the light bulb and the telephone, were working on such amazing devices as the phonograph, the motion picture camera, and the X-ray machine. People everywhere looked forward to the promising world of the new century.

However, change doesn't come just with the turn of a calendar page. It takes time for people to explore new ideas, act on them, and get used to them. Law enforcement was a case in point. In the first decade of the 20th century, police still relied on investigative methods pioneered by Scotland Yard in the 19th century.

CRIME REPORT

In the 1870s, it took Canada's "Great Detective," John Wilson Murray of Toronto, months to track down an elusive counterfeiter because he had to personally travel from city to city in search of clues. Technological advances in communications made in the early 20th century allowed Murray's successors to solve many crimes faster and with less legwork.

A PHOTOGRAPH AND A CLOTHES BRUSH

On June 28, 1909, Constable Isaac Decker of the British Columbia Provincial Police was shot dead in a confrontation with two suspected train robbers. One suspect was also killed, and the other one fled. Police found nothing on the dead suspect that could help identify him, except a clothes brush from a company in Long Beach, California, and a photograph of a little girl. The clothes brush indicated that the man was probably American. The Canadians sent the two clues, plus a photograph of the dead man, to the American police.

It took time and legwork, but with the help of the Long Beach Police Department, a detective found the Los Angeles photography studio where the picture of the girl had been taken. That led the detective to the home of a family named Haney. On the mantelpiece was a photograph of the suspect who had been killed in Canada. His name was Dave Haney. He and his brother Bill had long criminal records. Several months later, Bill Haney was captured while trying to rob a bank in Montana.

Thanks to two photographs and a clothes brush, the murder of Constable Decker was solved. But the success of the investigation was also due to good luck. Police would soon come to rely more on modern equipment and increasingly sophisticated methods of investigation than on lucky breaks.

CARS, CRIME LABS, AND COOPERATION

The early 20th century saw many technological developments that aided police work. An expanding telephone network enhanced communications. Advances in photography allowed police to have pictures of criminals, suspects, and missing persons reproduced in newspapers. But the greatest revolution in crime and crime fighting came with the automobile.

Criminals found that it was easy to drive into a small town in a stolen car, rob a bank, and then make a fast getaway. To combat the "automobile bandits," police departments made cars standard equipment. The cop in the patrol car became as common a sight as the cop walking his beat. The car radio gave police a major advantage over criminals. A police dispatcher could quickly direct cars to a crime scene. And when two-way radios became common, officers in trouble could immediately call for help.

Positive identification of criminals had long been a problem for police as well. The Bertillon system, developed in France in 1870, used photographs and body measurements to record information about convicted criminals, but was useless for investigative purposes. People had known about fingerprints for centuries, but nobody had ever used them in criminal investigations.

In 1897, Sir Edward Richard Henry, a British police commissioner, devised a system for classifying fingerprints. The Henry Method was a major development. It meant that a single fingerprint, or even a part of one, could connect a suspect to a crime.

In 1910 a French scientist named Edmond Locard established the world's first crime laboratory. His theory was, "Every contact leaves a trace." He meant that a criminal always takes something from a crime scene, and leaves something behind. This idea became the basic principle of forensic science. Locard examined such clues as hair, blood, threads from clothing, dirt

DENTAL DETECTION

Identifying a body by its teeth dates back to ancient Rome. But only since the early 20th century has *odontology* been scientifically applied in criminal cases. Dental records and bite marks have been used to identify human remains, and even convict suspected murderers. Many of the victims of the 9/11 terrorist attacks on New York City were identified through dental remains.

scraped from under fingernails, and mud stuck on shoes. Science was becoming the criminal investigator's greatest ally.

American law enforcement was slow to accept the new ideas. The first full-service crime lab in the United States wasn't established until 1929. The Scientific Crime Detection Laboratory in Chicago, Illinois, was a direct result of a gangland mass murder called the St. Valentine's Day Massacre. Calvin Goddard, a ballistics expert, connected bullets taken from the victims' bodies to a gun that had been used in other crimes. One of the killers was caught and sentenced to life in prison. Because of Goddard's fine work, his crime lab was expanded beyond the study of ballistics. By 1931, Goddard was teaching forensic science to future investigators.

Criminals often tried to escape arrest by fleeing to other countries. Most national governments had extradition agreements with their foreign counterparts, allowing them to bring criminals home. For example, in 1842, the Unites States and Great Britain signed the Webster-Ashburton Treaty, in which each agreed to arrest and repatriate any fugitives wanted for murder, robbery, piracy, arson, or forgery. This was to discourage criminals from border-hopping between the United States and Britain's North American colonies (now Canada).

As law enforcement grew more sophisticated, and criminals became more mobile, the need grew for increased international police cooperation. The International Criminal Police Commission (ICPC) was founded in Vienna, Austria, in 1923. However, in 1938 it fell under the domination of Nazi Germany. After World War II ended in 1945, it was revived as the International Criminal Police Organization (Interpol). With its headquarters in France, Interpol would eventually have a membership of more than 190 countries. Today, its worldwide fight against crime focuses on such issues as the drug trade, human trafficking, weapons smuggling, money laundering, and piracy.

In the United States, legal jurisdiction was divided between the federal and state governments. The various police departments didn't always cooperate. In fact, local and state police departments often resented "outsiders" intruding on their territory. Criminals took advantage of this situation, evading arrest simply by crossing a state line.

The first American experiment in cooperative crime control came in 1934 with the Five State Pact. The governors of Illinois, Indiana, Michigan, Ohio, and Minnesota agreed to allow each other's police to cross state lines in pursuit of criminals. One man who approved of this measure was J. Edgar Hoover.

THE FBI: A DEADLY GAME OF COPS AND ROBBERS

In the midst of the Great Depression of the 1930s, a crime wave swept across the United States. Desperadoes like George "Machine Gun" Kelly, Lester "Baby Face" Nelson, Charles "Pretty Boy" Floyd, and Public Enemy Number One, John Dillinger, went on a rampage of armed robbery and kidnapping. They shot many policemen who got in their way.

J. Edgar Hoover was the director of the Justice Department's Bureau of Investigation, a small federal police agency with limited authority. Its agents were not permitted to carry firearms. That changed after June 17, 1933, when gangsters killed a federal agent and three other policemen in Kansas City.

The federal government expanded the legal authority of Hoover's department and allowed the agents to be armed. Hoover declared a "war on crime" and sent his agents after the public enemies. A few criminals, like Machine Gun Kelly, were captured and sent to prison. Others, like

"MACHINE GUN" AND THE "G MEN"

FBI agents were nicknamed "G Men" (Government Men). A popular story attributed the name to Machine Gun Kelly, who allegedly cried, "Don't shoot, G Men!" when he was arrested. The story was actually fabricated, possibly by J. Edgar Hoover.

DEATH IN THE SKY

On November 1, 1955, a DC-6B airliner crashed near Denver, Colorado. All forty-four people on board were killed. The FBI turned an airplane hangar into a crime lab, and reassembled the plane from the wreckage. They found that the plane had been blown out of the sky by a bomb. Investigation led to John Gilbert Graham, who had hidden the bomb in his mother's luggage. He expected to cash in on life insurance policies. Graham was convicted of murder and executed in 1957.

Baby Face Nelson, chose to shoot it out. Nelson killed two agents before dying from gunshot wounds. Hoover's agents tracked down and killed Pretty Boy Floyd and John Dillinger.

Hoover made sure his department's successes received plenty of publicity. Soon he was recognized as a crime-fighting hero. His department was re-named the Federal Bureau of Investigation (FBI) in 1935. Not everybody liked Hoover, and some people questioned his methods and accused him of abusing his authority. Nonetheless, Hoover was credited with making the FBI into a highly efficient federal police force.

Today the FBI is one of the most formidable law enforcement agencies in the world. The FBI National Academy, founded in 1935, trains American and foreign police officials in up-to-date investigative techniques. FBI officers and support personnel number in the thousands, operating out of offices all over the United States. The FBI's state-of-the-art crime laboratory employs about five hundred scientists and agents. They are all part of the U.S.'s defense against terrorists, cybercrime, and the global illicit drug trade—dangers that didn't even exist when FBI agents first went after bandits like John Dillinger and Pretty Boy Floyd.

GETTING THE EVIDENCE

As the 20th century progressed, police departments had access to more and more specialized technology and scientific methods of fighting crime. For example, at one time the tools for finding and documenting fingerprints were simply a magnifying glass and a camera. By mid-century, however, the detective had a professional's kit that included aluminum and magnetic fingerprint powders, adhesive tape for "lifting" prints, brushes, ink rollers, labels, and specially designed fingerprint forms. Information on crimes and criminals was stored in organized files and on databases.

The expanding role that forensics played in criminal investigations meant that police laboratories had to expand their inventories beyond such basic items as fingerprints and bullets. Along with gathering a vast array of fibers, human and animal hair, and plant and insect specimens, major police departments also built up large collections of automotive paint samples. A fleck of a car's paint found at the scene of a fatal hit-and-run accident could tell police the make, model, and year of the vehicle involved, and help lead them to the owner.

Police consulted with people who were knowledgeable in a wide range of fields. Handwriting experts helped identify the authors of bank robbery notes and forged letters. Chemical engineers determined the substances used to manufacture a bomb.

EVERY CONTACT LEAVES A TRACE

In 1963, fingerprints found on a ketchup bottle and a Monopoly game led to the capture of the bandits who committed Britain's Great Train Robbery.

As early as 1904, investigators were able to determine that a greasy film found on the underside of leaves on a tree was human fat. This enabled the police to locate the spot where a suspected murderer had disposed of the victim's body by burning it. By the 1960s, forensics investigators could learn much about human remains through chemical analysis and studying the development of larvae and insects in the flesh. However, information provided by witnesses was still of vital importance. In some instances, investigators might compile a thick file of circumstantial evidence on a suspect, but would have little chance of getting a conviction in court if they had no witnesses—or if potential witnesses wouldn't testify.

A WRITTEN SELF-PORTRAIT

A series of bomb explosions in the summer of 1962 killed several people in Lucerne, Switzerland. The bombs had been planted in public places like restaurants. The investigation led police to a firearms dealer who had sold the detonators found in debris at the crime scenes. The man who had bought the detonators had signed the registration form as "Alfred Spani." Both the signature and the address written beside it were false.

With only this slim clue, police turned to M. Litsenow, the country's leading graphologist (handwriting expert). He agreed to help, although he doubted he'd be able to tell much about the suspect from such a small sample.

After analyzing the registration form, Litsenow told the police that the man they were looking for was of average intelligence, not well educated, and about twenty years old, with an unstable personality. He was most likely a loner, a casual laborer, and athletic. He probably knew somebody named Alfred, and had some connection with the false address. There might have been alcoholism in his family, and his parents were probably separated.

TRACKS IN THE SAND

Scottish pathologist Sir Sydney Smith was an advisor to the Egyptian government in the 1920s. He helped solve the murder of a victim whose body was found in the desert by hiring Bedouin tribesmen who were experts at reading tracks in the sand. The trackers led police to a suspect, and Smith proved through ballistics that the suspect's rifle was the murder weapon.

Most likely the family had been involved with social services and the suspect had been in minor trouble with the police.

The police focused their information on a handful of suspects. They dismissed all but one: twenty-year-old Anton Fahndrich. Amazingly, he matched almost every detail of Litsenow's profile, including being a poorly educated loner with alcoholic parents.

Fahndrich confessed to the bombings. He said he had a need to "revenge himself on society," and that he became excited by the sound of the explosions, the shouts of the people, and the wail of police sirens. He had never thought that a few words written on a registration form would provide police with his self-portrait.

CRACKING THE KRAY CASE

Twin brothers Reginald and Ronald Kray were notorious criminals in London's tough East End. They extorted money from their victims, and were feared because of their reputation for using extreme violence. People who opposed them in any way were savagely beaten or murdered. Police were aware of the Krays' criminal activities, but found that people were too afraid of them to talk.

In 1967, the senior officials at Scotland Yard quietly put Superintendent Leonard "Nipper" Read in charge of the Kray investigation. Secrecy was necessary, because it was suspected that some police officers were accepting bribes from the Krays. Read put together a handpicked team of detectives he could trust.

For months Superintendent Read and his men gathered evidence against the Krays. Their greatest obstacle was the wall of silence they met in the East End. Meanwhile, the Krays became aware of the investigation and issued threats. In a later interview, Read said, "We were all family men and so had to look over our shoulders and vary our routes to work for fear of hits." ("Hit" is a street term for murder.)

Slowly, witnesses began to talk to the detectives. People in the East End were becoming alarmed at the Krays' excessive violence and behavior that bordered on insanity. They were willing to talk if Read could guarantee them police protection. Read even learned that the brothers had offered a large reward for anyone who would kill him.

Far from being intimidated, Read continued with the investigation efficiently and patiently. A break came when the Krays told a man named Alan Cooper to kill a rival gangster. Cooper passed the job on to another man, Paul Elvey. Read's men had been watching Elvey, and caught him in illegal possession of explosives, with which he intended to commit the murder. Under questioning, Elvey gave up Cooper's name. Cooper in turn told Read that the murder plot had begun with the Krays, and that he was willing to testify against them.

By May 9, 1968, Read's team had enough evidence and witnesses for the Krays to be prosecuted for murder. Once the terrible twins were behind bars, even more witnesses came forward. Superintendent Read's excellent police work sent the Krays to prison for life.

FIGHTING ORGANIZED CRIME

One of the greatest challenges to law enforcement in the first half of the 20th century was the rise of organized crime, which was known in the United States by such names as the Mob, la Cosa Nostra, the Syndicate, and the Mafia. Powerful Italian-American crime bosses like Charles "Lucky" Luciano of New York ran their illicit operations like corporations. They established shadowy empires based on extortion, bootlegging, drug dealing, gambling, prostitution, and loan-sharking (lending money at very high interest rates). They used intimidation and profits from these illegal activities to move in on legitimate businesses.

Organized crime bosses, or "dons," as some were called, preferred secrecy to newspaper headlines. They would hire thugs to do their dirty work so they couldn't be held personally responsible for crimes of violence. They took advantage of every legal angle available to protect themselves from the police, and employed the best lawyers money could buy. Whenever a gangster was arrested, his lawyer would quickly bail him out.

One of the major difficulties in fighting organized crime was the refusal of many top lawmen, including J. Edgar Hoover, to even admit that it existed in the United States. However, other officials, like Attorney General Thomas Dewey, recognized the growing power of the mobsters and tried to do something about it. In 1936, Dewey had more than a hundred suspects associated with Lucky Luciano arrested. He had a judge set their bail so high that many of them couldn't afford to get out of jail. Some of them were minor figures in Luciano's organization, but they had information about his criminal activities, and they began to talk. This led to Luciano's arrest and imprisonment.

Twenty years later, senior police officials still denied the existence of the Mafia. Then, on November 14, 1957, more than a hundred gangsters from cities across the United States, as well as from Canada and Italy, held a "summit" meeting at the country home of Mafia boss Joseph Barbara outside the little town of Apalachin, New York. Local police grew suspicious of the large number of big expensive cars with out-of-state license plates converging on such a tiny, out-of-the-way community. They set up roadblocks and then raided the meeting. Many of the participants fled into the woods surrounding the estate, but the police managed to catch fifty-eight Mafia bosses and charge them with a variety of offenses. The large gathering of senior Mafia dons removed any doubt that organized crime did in fact exist in the United States.

To get around the code of *omerta* (silence) that forbade any Mafia member from turning informer, police employed an arsenal of electronic surveillance devices. By the 1960s, these included cameras, microphones, tape recorders, transmitters, and receivers. Police were legally authorized to use listening devices called bugs to eavesdrop on the conversations of known gangsters.

Planting a bug in a place where it would be effective could be very dangerous. Mobsters were suspicious of anyone caught snooping around their homes, offices, or hangouts. Sometimes a police agent would go to the location in disguise and get in by deception. One undercover cop gained entry to a gangster's house

by posing as a home repairman. The most obvious place to conceal a bug was the telephone, but since gangsters often suspected that their phones were "tapped," agents had to be resourceful and find other hiding spots for the devices. This particular agent sneaked into the bedroom and was installing a bug under the bed when the gangster suddenly walked in. The officer was sure he'd be shot before another minute passed. But the unsuspecting gangster simply told him to finish whatever repair he was making and get out, because he wanted to take a nap.

As hazardous as it was to place bugs in gangsters' homes and other strategic locations, an undercover police agent's most dangerous task was to pose as a criminal and infiltrate a gang. In 1976, FBI agent Joseph Pistone did just that. Pistone's family background was Sicilian and he spoke fluent Italian. As a boy he had become familiar with the mannerisms of the local gangsters in his neighborhood in Paterson, New Jersey. Pistone played the part so well that what was supposed to be a six-month assignment became six years of dangerous deception.

Pretending to be an expert jewel thief named Donnie Brasco, Pistone worked his way into the confidence of the Bonanno and Colombo Mafia "families." Only a few FBI agents knew who "Donnie Brasco" really was. While secretly gathering information, Pistone had to be on guard every moment. If he were caught wearing a "wire" (a listening device hidden under his clothing), if someone from his "real" life recognized him while he was in the company of gangsters, or if he made the slightest slip that would arouse the suspicions of the criminals he was spying on, it would cost him his life.

"Donnie Brasco" proved to be an intelligence gold mine for the FBI. He opened a window into the inner workings of the Mafia. His information led to more than a hundred convictions of Mafia members. Angry Mafia dons put a $500,000 "contract" on Pistone's life, but withdrew it after warnings from the FBI. Nonetheless, Pistone traveled in disguise and under an assumed name. He stayed away from any place that had a strong Mafia presence.

Continued electronic and undercover surveillance helped American law enforcement agencies to arrest more top Mafia bosses. One was John Gotti. He was called "the Teflon Don" because police had been unable to make criminal charges against him "stick." In 1990, FBI bugs in a New York social club recorded Gotti's boasts about people he'd had "whacked" (murdered). Gotti was sent to prison, and died there in 2002.

Organized crime has never been completely stamped out. Like a virus, it evolves and adapts. The old-time mobsters gave way to international crime cartels dealing in drugs and arms. And the surveillance devices police use to keep track of the mobsters' activities have also evolved, from simple bugs to computer and satellite technology.

THE MIRACLE OF DNA

"DNA" is the short name given to the molecular genetic code that is in every living organism. Although it is passed from parents to children, every single person's DNA is unique. Scientific study of DNA dates back to the 19th century, but it wasn't until 1985 that DNA "fingerprinting" was developed. For police, this was the biggest breakthrough in forensics in over a century.

DNA can be extracted from any bodily tissue or fluid, and it has many scientific uses. For police investigative purposes, DNA is usually taken from blood, saliva, and other bodily fluids, as well as

A TINY DIFFERENCE IS ALL IT TAKES

Deoxyribonucleic acid (DNA) is in almost every cell of the human body. About 98 percent of the DNA structure in your cells is the same as that of every other human being. But tiny differences make your DNA as unique as your fingerprints.

skin and hair. It can be used in the investigation of a wide range of crimes, from robbery to assault and murder. A criminal might wear gloves to avoid leaving fingerprints, but still leave behind hairs, or saliva on something like a cigarette butt.

DNA testing has been used to identify human remains that are no longer recognizable. Many homicide cases that had been "cold" for years have been solved through DNA testing. One was the murder of eighty-year-old Rosa Cinnamon in Portland, Oregon, in 1976. She was strangled and beaten to death in her apartment. Traces of blood and skin found under her fingernails showed that she had fought her attacker. The samples were stored away, and the crime went unsolved for thirty-three years.

In 2007, Cold Case Unit investigator Robbie Thompson resubmitted evidence from the Cinnamon murder to a crime lab. In January of the following year, she was informed that the DNA taken from the fingernail scrapings matched that of a man who had died in prison in 2003 while serving a life term for a double murder committed in 1979. He had a long criminal record, and was living in Mrs. Cinnamon's neighborhood at the time of her murder.

DNA testing has also been instrumental in proving the innocence of many people wrongfully convicted of crimes such as murder and assault. David Brian Dougherty of New Zealand was convicted in 1993 on charges of kidnapping and assaulting his neighbor. He spent three years in prison before DNA fingerprinting ruled him out as the perpetrator. A documentary film called *Until Proven Innocent* was made about his case.

In the United States, a program called the Innocence Project, which was established in 1992, uses DNA and other evidence to re-examine the cases of people convicted of major crimes. It has successfully proven the innocence of more than two hundred individuals. Fourteen of them were men on death row, awaiting execution for murder.

CHAPTER 7

WOMEN WEAR THE BADGE

POLICING WAS ONCE CONSIDERED TO BE STRICTLY "MEN'S WORK." Back then, many considered women to be "the weaker sex" and "too emotional." However, in the mid-19th century, police departments began hiring women as jail matrons to administer to female and juvenile prisoners. In the United States, the matrons were often the widows of deceased police officers. The job was a sort of unofficial death benefit—a way to help women who no longer had husbands to support their families.

Around the turn of the 20th century, Mary Owens of Chicago, Illinois, and Lola Baldwin of Portland, Oregon, were the first American women to officially serve as police officers. They worked mostly with women and children. Alice Stebbins Wells is generally recognized as the first American to be called a police*woman*. A social worker who joined the Los Angeles Police Department (LAPD) in 1910, Wells was a visionary who wanted to help women and children who were victims of crime. She believed that a modern police department had to have a feminine influence.

By the time of World War I, women had also joined police departments in Canada, the United Kingdom, and Australia. In the U.K., this was partly due to the war. So many policemen had enlisted in the British armed forces that police departments were understaffed. However, the main reason women were breaking the gender barrier into police work was a recognition, often reluctant on the part of male administrations, of the need for a female presence in policing.

Male cops weren't supposed to be social workers. Some police chiefs even considered such work a waste of time and taxpayers' money. However, the more forward-thinking chiefs realized that crime levels were lower when social issues like poverty and alcohol abuse were addressed. Still, they generally considered social work less important than "real" police work, and thought women were more suited to it than men because of their "mothering instinct."

The first policewomen were therefore restricted to being morals officers, working mainly with women and juveniles. In London, England, the Women Police Service founded in 1914 by Margaret Damer Dawson and Nina Boyle concentrated its efforts on rescuing young women from prostitution and discouraging boys and girls in poor neighborhoods from turning to crime. Policewomen in other countries had similar duties. They supervised dancehalls

FIRST LADY OF THE LAW

In recognition of Alice Stebbins Wells's place as America's first policewoman, the Los Angeles Police Department gave her a special badge that honored her as Policewoman Number One. She wore it on formal occasions with a dress uniform she had made herself from the drab, blue LAPD uniform.

that were popular with young people, and acted as street-level counselors for abandoned wives, unwed mothers, and runaway teenagers. They escorted female prisoners between jail and court. The first policewomen in Toronto, Canada, Mary Minty and Maria Levitt, even had the unusual assignment of enforcing rules that regulated fortune-tellers. In some parts of the United States, policewomen could "rescue" prostitutes, but only male officers could arrest them if they persisted in their illegal activities.

The policewomen themselves had to adhere to a strict moral code. Any "improper" behavior could result in dismissal. In Australia, only single women could join the Women Police Branch, and they had to resign if they got married. It wasn't considered acceptable for a woman to work at a full-time career if she had a family home to maintain.

Women still faced old prejudices, too. One concern was that women who wanted to be police officers were likely to be involved with "militant feminist causes," such as fighting for women's right to vote. Another objection was that female police officers took away jobs from men who had families to support.

FROM SOCIAL WORK TO CHIEF OF POLICE

It wasn't until after World War II that policewomen emerged as front-line crime fighters. They became part of mainstream policing, rather than having separate "women's" departments. Female officers began walking beats and riding in patrol cars. They proved that they could effectively handle the worst that the meanest streets could offer. But it took a long time to dispel the notion that women couldn't be good cops. Many people clung to the myth that women were too emotional and not physically strong enough for the job. Some male officers objected to working with women and subjected female officers to workplace harassment. Even today, there are people who, because of political, religious, or cultural prejudices, believe that women should not be police officers.

In spite of such opposition, women have made tremendous advances in policing since the time of Alice Stebbins Wells. Women are employed by departments all over the world as constables, detectives, and specialists in every facet of scientific investigation. Even in traditionally male-dominated societies, like those of Yemen

MALE COPS VERSUS FEMALE COPS

Female police officers are often compared unfavorably to their male colleagues. Because women don't always have the same physical strength as men, some people believed that police departments lowered their standards by allowing women to join. However, in the United States, studies by the National Center for Women and Policing have shown that female officers are eight times less likely than male officers to be involved in civilian complaints about the use of excessive force, even though they are far more likely to face vulgar and abusive language. That means fewer civil legal actions brought against the department.

and Iran, police departments have female officers. Saudi Arabia recently allowed women to become constables, but they can only participate in the investigation and arrest of female suspects. Since 1985, when Penny Harrington of Portland, Oregon, became the first female chief of police in the United States, dozens of American cities have had a woman as top cop. Canada, Norway, Denmark, Liberia, Guatemala, Nicaragua, and the Czech Republic are among the many other countries in which there have been female chiefs of police.

The rise in the number of women police officers in countries like the United States, Canada, and the United Kingdom has been slow but steady. A 1971 survey showed that only 1.4 percent of all American police officers were women. By 2013 the figure had crept up to 13 percent. That figure mostly represented women in the lower police ranks—just 2 percent of American police chiefs were women—but it shows a significant jump in numbers.

ON THE FIRING LINE

As "social workers," the first policewomen weren't given the tough, unpleasant, potentially dangerous jobs assigned to male officers. The attitude still prevailed that women couldn't be as effective as men in rough situations, and had to be shielded from the worst aspects of crime, such as grisly murder scenes. Over time women on the force proved that attitude wrong, though it has never entirely gone away.

Although many policewomen still work with females and juveniles, they are now part of the front line in the fight against crime, where they are at risk of personal injury—or worse. Some have had their achievements officially recognized, and a few have made the ultimate sacrifice.

On January 12, 2010, six armed men robbed a bank in Birmingham, England. Constables Catherine Jane Morgan, Kate Peplow, and Diana Shaw of the West Midlands Police were in a car, unarmed, on a routine patrol when they were informed by radio of a suspected robbery. They responded immediately.

In the encounter that followed, two of the suspects pointed guns at them. Peplow swung her arm to knock aside a gun that was aimed at her head. The robbers fled, and the constables gave chase on foot. They followed the suspects into what appeared to be a dead end—an especially risky move since cornered armed criminals can be the most dangerous of all.

The gunmen managed to slip away under the cover of darkness, but evidence the policewomen gathered at the crime scene led to the arrest of all six suspects. The unarmed policewomen had risked their lives to protect the public. For their courage and commitment to duty, PCs Peplow, Morgan, and Shaw were awarded the International Association of Women Police (IAWP) Medal of Valor in 2011.

Officer Jillian Michelle Smith of Arlington, Texas, was just two weeks out of field training when on December 28, 2010, she was dispatched to what should have been a routine call. A man known to be a violent offender had threatened his ex-girlfriend in her home. He had allegedly left the premises, and Officer Smith was only expected to take the woman's statement.

While she was still there, however, the man returned with a gun. As he opened fire, Officer Smith threw herself between the gun and the woman's eleven-year-old daughter. Smith was killed, but the girl escaped from the apartment. The gunman killed the woman, and then shot himself. In 2011, Officer Jillian Smith was posthumously awarded the IAWP Medal of Valor.

TWO COURAGEOUS POLICEWOMEN

While women in some nations have made great strides in policing, in other parts of the world they have only recently begun to overcome social and traditional barriers. In some developing nations, policing in general lags behind because law enforcement agencies are poorly funded. They lack facilities and equipment, and actual police training is sometimes almost nonexistent. Male officers often have priority for available resources, too. And in some countries women are held back because of firmly entrenched religious beliefs. Even if the government of a religiously conservative country authorizes the enlistment of female police officers, there is often strong resentment against the officers among some parts of the population.

FIRST TO FALL

In 1916, Anna Hart, a matron with the sheriff's department in Hamilton, Ohio, was murdered by a prisoner who was attempting to escape. She was the first American female law enforcement officer to be killed in the line of duty.

But there are always women who are working to change those attitudes. Shahzadi Gulfam joined the Pakistani Punjab Police Force in 1985. She came from a remote village with patriarchal traditions, and decided, against heavy odds, to become a policewoman. In 1997, Officer Gulfam became the first female police officer from Pakistan to be assigned to the United Nations Police (UNPOL). She worked in dangerous places like Bosnia and Kosovo, and then was sent to Timor-Leste, where she was a police commander. Then she became the UNPOL team leader with the Vulnerable Persons Unit (VPU), and solved many cases involving victims of abuse and assault. Her job was particularly difficult because many victims of domestic violence were reluctant to talk to police. Gulfam carried out public awareness programs and improved the VPU by making its facilities more comfortable for children. In 2011, Shahzadi Gulfam was the recipient of the United Nations International Female Police Peacekeeper Award.

Unfortunately, there have been instances in which a woman's advancement in policing has ended tragically. Malalai Kakar knew the dangers when she joined the Afghanistan police force in 1985. Many people still clung to ancient traditions that forbade women from doing anything that was considered men's work. Kakar was soon attacked by three gunmen. She shot and killed them in self-defense.

In 1995, Kakar was forced to leave the police force when Afghanistan came under the oppressive rule of the Taliban, a group of religious extremists. Then, in 2001, the Taliban regime was toppled, and a new government was established with the help of the United States and its allies. Kakar was called back to police duties.

Kakar became a symbol of hope to Afghan women. She headed a unit that investigated crimes against women. She once rescued a wife and her young daughter who were being kept in a cage.

Kakar was promoted to lieutenant-colonel, making her the highest ranking policewoman in Afghanistan. She was popular among the Afghan people, and foreign journalists wrote about her. But all this attracted the attention of the Taliban, who had launched a war of terrorism to regain power. The Taliban sent death threats to Kakar and her family. She defiantly refused to be intimidated.

On September 28, 2008, Kakar was in a car driven by her son Farhad when gunmen opened fire, killing them both. The Taliban boasted about the attack. The rest of the world denounced it as the murder of a courageous policewoman. Lieutenant-Colonel Malalai Kakar remains a symbol of hope to the women of Afghanistan.

CRIME REPORT

In June 2008, Taliban assassins murdered Bibi Hoor, making her the first Afghan policewoman to be killed in the line of duty. Malalai Kakar knew she could be next, but she wouldn't let herself be intimidated by the Taliban.

Worldwide, policewomen are still overcoming challenges and working hard to make a difference in their communities. Besides fighting crime as front-line constables on the street, women work in such specialized areas as forensics. Clea Koff, a British-born American forensic anthropologist, worked for the United Nations International Criminal Tribunal from 1996 to 2000 in Rwanda, Bosnia, Serbia, Croatia, and Kosovo. She helped in the identification of victims of genocide (mass murder of a racial or ethnic group), and gathered evidence against those responsible for the crimes.

Women have also, in a sense, come full circle from their days as "social workers" to now be seen as crime prevention experts, whose work with society's most vulnerable citizens not only improves the quality of people's lives, but lowers the crime rate and makes communities safer.

CRIME WRITER

Forensic anthropologist Clea Koff wrote about her work in her book *The Bone Woman: Among the Dead in Rwanda, Bosnia, Croatia and Kosovo*, which was published in 2004. Koff inherited a strong interest in human rights from her parents, and knew while still a teenager that she wanted to study osteology (the science of bones) and anthropology (the science dealing with the physical and cultural development of humans). She was analyzing prehistoric skeletons in California when the UN asked her to join a small team of scientists in Rwanda.

One amazing story comes from South Africa. For many years the black population of that nation suffered under the oppression of a racist system called apartheid. The South African Police was the government's principal agency for enforcing its policies of racial discrimination. Women were allowed to join the police force in the 1970s, but like the male officers, they had to be white.

The apartheid system collapsed in 1994 with the election of Nelson Mandela as the first black president of South Africa. Mandela encouraged black citizens to apply for the police force that they had previously feared and hated. One recruit was Olga Njengabo Masetla, who joined the department in 2002. Masetla started out as a patrol cop and graduated to crime scene investigator. She was instrumental in the arrests of numerous suspects. But it was through her work as a Social Crime Prevention Coordinator that Officer Masetla stood out, and in 2012 she received the IAWP Award for Community Service.

Masetla's tireless efforts on behalf of needy children, low-income mothers, and the elderly and disabled displayed vision and resourcefulness. Among her many projects were a daycare center where children learned about the dangers of crime, a cottage industry in which people with handicaps made artifacts that could be sold to tourists, and even Olga's Book Club, which improved literacy among children and helped steer them away from street gangs. Officer Masetla's work showed that "social work" as a means of crime prevention had come a long way since the days of Alice Stebbins Wells and Margaret Damer Dawson.

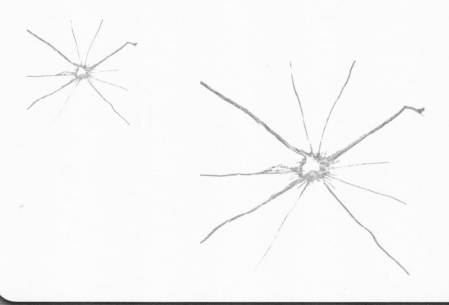

CHAPTER 8

BAD COPS

FROM 1920 TO 1933, A LAW CALLED PROHIBITION MADE THE SALE of alcoholic beverages illegal in the United States. Gangsters quickly took over the alcohol business, smuggling in beer and liquor, and even manufacturing it themselves. Criminals like Chicago's Al Capone made so much money they could "buy off" police. Thousands of dishonest law enforcement officers, from customs agents and ordinary patrolmen to chiefs of police, were "on the take": accepting bribes to let gangsters operate without interference. Crooked cops contributed to the failure of Prohibition.

Corrupt officers have been a problem as long as there have been laws. From ancient times to the present, there have been officers whose weak ethics have been overcome by greed and ambition. All over the world, criminals pay police to allow the flow of illicit drugs along international routes. In some developing nations where the urban crime rate is high, wealthy citizens and business owners pay off-duty

MOONLIGHTING

During Chicago's "Beer Wars" of the 1920s, police officers in the pay of gangsters like Al Capone and his chief rival, Bugs Moran, escorted convoys of trucks loaded with illegal alcohol to protect them from hijackers.

At gangster warehouses, the officers would help the bootleggers unload the trucks.

THE WRONG MAN

Henry Plummer of Montana was another lawman who met a terrible fate. In 1864, a vigilante mob accused Sheriff Plummer of being the leader of a bandit gang, and hanged him along with several other suspected outlaws. For many years Plummer was regarded as a classic example of a lawman gone bad. However, modern historians who have studied Plummer's case believe he may have been innocent.

police officers to form death squads that go into slum areas to "exterminate" suspected thieves. Many of their victims are street people who steal to survive.

Rogue cops have been known to abuse their authority in order to intimidate people or make personal gains. They might even frame a suspect in order to officially "solve" a highly publicized crime.

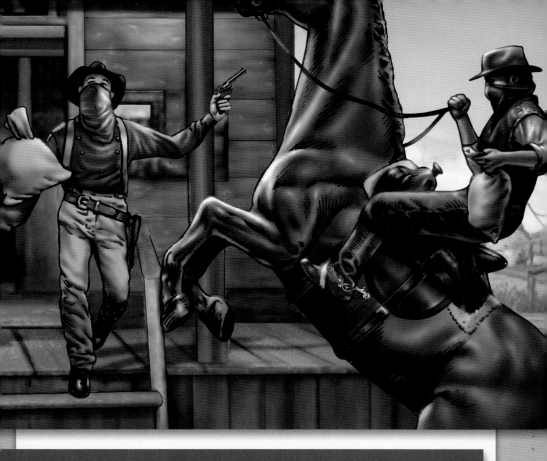

A LAWMAN GOES BAD

 Henry Brown was a noted gunslinger who became the marshal of Caldwell, Kansas, in 1882. Caldwell was a rip-roaring cowtown where three former marshals had already died "with their boots on" (an Old West expression that meant a person died violently). The citizens thought that a fast gun like Brown was just what they needed to establish law and order. Marshal Brown quickly tamed Caldwell. After he shot two outlaws foolish enough to tangle with him, would-be troublemakers behaved themselves, and desperadoes stayed away. The local newspaper praised Brown as the best officer of the law in the West.

Unfortunately, Brown was a big spender and had growing debts. There were several ways in which corrupt Old West lawmen could make money illegally. Some skimmed off the taxes they collected. Others accepted bribes from illegal gambling operations. Henry Brown chose armed robbery. He believed that his position as a respected lawman was the perfect cover—no one would suspect him.

Under the ruse of leaving Caldwell to track down an outlaw, Brown rode to the town of Medicine Lodge. There, he and three other men attempted to rob the bank. They killed two men, and were captured after a blazing gunfight with a posse. Brown was shot dead when he tried to escape. The people of Caldwell were stunned by the news, and felt that Brown had betrayed them and the office with which they had entrusted him.

FRANK SERPICO: CRUSADE AGAINST CORRUPTION

In the 1960s, Frank Serpico was a New York City police officer who worked the streets undercover. He investigated criminals involved in drug dealing and vice. Serpico was a "clean cop" who wouldn't accept bribes. However, he saw that some of his colleagues were "dirty cops" who took bribes and even pocketed evidence.

In 1967, Serpico submitted a formal report on the police corruption he had witnessed. His superiors ignored it. For four years Serpico tried using official police channels in his anti-corruption crusade, and got nowhere.

MOVIE HERO
Frank Serpico's story was dramatized in the 1973 movie *Serpico* starring Al Pacino.

Frustrated with the police department's failure to take action, Serpico went to the *New York Times* in 1970. The newspaper's sensational story resulted in the mayor forming an official commission to investigate police corruption in New York City.

Serpico received death threats. He was assaulted by other officers. But he refused to be intimidated, and continued to work as an undercover investigator.

On the night of February 3, 1971, Serpico and three other officers went to an apartment on what was supposed to be a drug bust. As Serpico attempted to force his way into the apartment, his colleagues abandoned him, leaving him to face armed drug dealers alone. Serpico was shot in the face and fell to the floor, where he lay bleeding. An elderly tenant who lived next door to the suspects' apartment called for an ambulance.

TWO FACES OF CORRUPTION

The Knapp Commission, which investigated corruption in the NYPD in the 1970s, divided dishonest officers into two groups. Cops who aggressively misused their authority for personal gain were called "meat eaters." Officers who simply accepted payoffs that came their way were called "grass eaters." Both were guilty of betraying the trust that had been placed in them.

Serpico survived to testify in hearings that exposed widespread corruption in the New York Police Department (NYPD). He was awarded the NYPD's Medal of Honor. Unfortunately, the gunshot had permanently deafened his right ear, and bone fragments in his brain gave him chronic headaches. Serpico left the police department in 1972, but continued to speak out against police corruption.

THE DEATH SQUADS OF RIO

Police departments in developing countries are often riddled with corruption because the pay is so low. An ordinary constable might be paid less than the equivalent of US$100 a month. In order to provide for their families, some officers make extra money by charging business owners a weekly fee for "special" protection from thieves, requesting rewards from homeowners for responding to reported robberies, and collecting on-the-spot "fines" from motorists. Sometimes a person who has broken the law will pay the police to look the other way and let them go.

This sort of official corruption has practically been a way of life for generations in parts of Latin America, Africa, and Asia, where some of the poorest countries in the world are located. Nobody complains, because that would invite trouble. However, police officers in one country went far beyond extortion and accepting bribes.

Rio de Janeiro and other major cities in Brazil are surrounded by huge slums called *favelas*. Unemployment in these squalid neighborhoods is high. Even many people who have jobs are poor, because the sweatshops in which they work long hours making things like clothing and shoes pay them very little money. Under the crushing poverty of the favelas, desperate people turn to crime to survive. They steal, or they join gangs that traffic in illegal drugs. They must live by their wits and their toughness in a world of mean streets. For some, the criminal life begins when they are very young, and they have little hope of ever finding their way out of it.

For a long time the local police were not very effective in dealing with criminals from the favelas in the conventional way.

Burglaries and armed robberies were epidemic. Even when thieves were caught, they were often released with a warning because Brazil's prisons were overcrowded. Shopkeepers and homeowners who were the most frequent victims of crime became impatient. They decided to do something about the problem themselves.

The solution, as angry businesspeople and property owners saw it, was vigilante justice. They hired armed men to go into the favelas at night to hunt down and kill any street people they suspected of being thieves. Many of the men in these posses were off-duty policemen looking for easy money. The bounty for a dead thief was the equivalent of about US$50.

Usually an accused thief who fell into the hands of a death squad was shot. In the 1980s and 1990s, when the death squad terror was at its height, thousands of street people were executed. None of the vigilantes were charged. The public considered them *justiceiros* (bringers of justice).

However, there were people in Brazil and other countries who saw the murders as an atrocity. After the mass slaying of eight youths in their sleep one night in 1993, the Brazilian government was pressured into taking action. The resulting investigation brought out even more stories of police criminality.

One young man who was shot and left for dead survived. The Brazilian government sent him to Switzerland for protection while the investigation continued. In 1996 he was returned to Rio de Janeiro under heavy guard to testify at the trials of three policemen who were

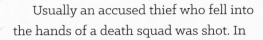

WAR ON DRUGS

Because of its geographic location, Mexico is a principal source of illegal drugs smuggled into the United States. The American and Mexican governments have cooperated for years in a "war on drugs" to stop the flow. However, powerful Mexican criminal organizations called cartels bribed and intimidated underpaid Mexican police officers. In 2006, Mexico's president, Felipe Calderón, called on the armed forces to assist in fighting the cartels, and began a reorganization of the police. In spite of Calderón's efforts, police corruption continued. In 2010, more than three thousand police officers were fired. The Mexican military has had to play an increasing role in fighting the cartels.

charged with the 1993 mass murder. The policemen were found guilty and sentenced to long prison terms. (Within a few years, however, two of them were released.)

The prosecution of the officers brought about a decline in the activities of the death squads, but it didn't end them. Poor people still steal to survive in the favelas. Underfunded social agencies still struggle to deal with the problem. And some underpaid officers still hire themselves out as vigilantes. However, organizations like Amnesty International are trying to end their activities for good, and many police officials are making an effort to cooperate with programs designed to assist Rio's poorest citizens.

FIRE THEM ALL!

When Mikheil Saakashvili became president of Georgia, a country in Eastern Europe, in 2004, one of the biggest problems he faced was official corruption. This was especially true of the Georgian National Police, which had about thirty-five thousand officers. Under previous administrations, the police were very poorly paid. They had to buy their own uniforms. The traffic police even had to pay for their patrol cars and gasoline. The government expected them to go out on the streets and raise money.

The traffic police were little more than bandits who extorted money from motorists along city streets and country highways. Anybody who refused to pay an officer risked being arrested, beaten up, or even having their car confiscated. The officers were obliged to turn a portion of the money over to their superiors.

Officers who were supposed to fight crime regularly took bribes. Torture was the most common means of getting confessions and information out of suspects. The public therefore hated and mistrusted the police. Many crimes went unreported because people didn't want to get involved with police thugs.

Saakashvili wanted to put an end to that. He raised police pay and urged officers to do their jobs honestly. But corrupt cops had been making so much money on the street that his attempt at reform didn't work. In 2005 the president took drastic action. He fired almost the entire police department—about twenty-five thousand people.

Saakashvili replaced the corrupt police with new recruits who had been trained by instructors from the U.S. State Department's Bureau of International Narcotics and Law Enforcement Affairs. Convincing applicants to come forward wasn't easy at first, because the police department had such a bad reputation. But the government provided the new officers with uniforms and a fleet of blue-and-white cars, and paid for the fuel. An officer's salary was now twenty times what it had been under the old system, so it was no longer necessary for the police to rob citizens. Saakashvili further improved the public image of the police when he outlawed the use of torture.

Police officers who were educated, better trained, and fairly paid made a big difference in Georgia. The crime rate went down, even though more crimes were being reported as the police gained the public trust. As one government official put it, "People actually like the police now. It shows people that the very worst part of our society could be reformed. It shows them there's hope."

CRIME REPORT

In the 1990s a scandal shook the Los Angeles Police Department. Dozens of officers in the Rampart Division were suspected of involvement with drug dealers and other criminals. The officers' offenses included robbery, assault, framing innocent people, destruction of evidence, and perjury. Of the fifty-eight officers who were tried, five were fired, seven resigned, and twelve were placed on suspension.

CHAPTER 9

SECRET POLICE

SECRET POLICE ORGANIZATIONS HAVE ALWAYS BEEN OBJECTS OF the deepest dread. They have lurked in the shadows of history since ancient times. Darius the Great of Persia had royal spies called "the Eyes and Ears of the King." Informers called *frumentarii* whispered in the ears of Roman emperors. In ancient China, Wu Zetian, the only woman who ever ruled there as empress, created a body of secret police who helped her strengthen her hold on power. In the Middle Ages, the royal courts of Europe and Asia were nests of intrigue in which a wrong word overheard by a monarch's secret agent could mean a death sentence. Centuries later, Russian czars relied on a secret police department called the Third Section to "watch the people." In the suspicion-haunted world of absolute rulers, secret police were a sinister reality.

THE INQUISITION

The Inquisition was a secret police organization that operated across Europe on behalf of the Catholic Church, starting in the 12th century. In an age of religious strife that lasted for hundreds of years, the Inquisition used spies and informers to root out heretics—people who didn't accept the pope's rulings on what constituted the Church's definition of correct Christian beliefs. Heretics were burned at the stake, as were people convicted of witchcraft.

Secret police, also known as intelligence agencies, have also been a necessity, although an uncomfortable one, in democratic societies. Conventional police methods couldn't pierce the dark cloak of silence and fear that protected crime syndicates, and later, terrorist organizations. It became necessary for law enforcement officers to go undercover to detect criminal acts and gather evidence on suspects. However, there have to be safeguards to ensure that secretive police activities don't infringe on people's democratic rights.

THE GESTAPO: AGENTS OF EVIL

In 1933, Adolf Hitler and the Nazi party came to power in Germany. The Nazis were fascists, and believed in absolute government control over people's lives. They had extremely racist views, and regarded all non-German people as inferior. They especially hated Jews, whom they scorned as "sub-human."

The Nazis turned Germany into a police state. To enforce Hitler's rule, they established the Gestapo, one of the most terrifying secret police organizations in history. It didn't exist to serve and protect the public, but to apprehend anyone considered an enemy of the Nazis. Gestapo tools were secrecy, betrayal, brutality, and fear. Under the command of Heinrich Himmler, one of Hitler's senior aides, the Gestapo was not regulated by any German laws. As far as the Nazis were concerned, the will of Hitler, Germany's *führer* (leader), *was* the law.

Operating out of their headquarters in Berlin, Gestapo agents spread throughout Germany to eliminate all opposition to Hitler.

Members of other political parties, writers, teachers, university professors, union leaders, clergymen, artists, students, anyone who disagreed with Hitler was arrested and sent to prisons called concentration camps. People lived in fear of a knock on the door in the dead of night. The terror was greatest among Germany's Jews, who were being rounded up and sent to overcrowded, heavily guarded districts called ghettos. There they waited in hunger, disease, and despair while the Nazis decided what to do with them.

Through propaganda and the offer of rewards, the Gestapo encouraged citizens to spy on their neighbors and denounce those who showed any sign of not conforming to Nazism. If you laughed at a joke about Hitler, or if you expressed sympathy for the Jews, you could be reported. Then the Gestapo would come for you.

The Gestapo presented itself to the German people as a disciplined, patriotic police force that worked in the best interests of the nation. The Nazi government said that people who were picked up on the street or snatched from their homes were simply being placed in "protective custody." But behind the walls of Gestapo headquarters and police buildings was a world of sheer horror.

DEFYING THE GESTAPO

In cities like Dusseldorf and Cologne, German teenagers who opposed Hitler formed gangs called the Edelweiss Pirates. They engaged in a dangerous game of cat-and-mouse with the Gestapo, painting anti-Hitler slogans on buildings and helping people who were hiding from the Nazis. Edelweiss Pirates who got caught were executed or sent to concentration camps.

Prisoners held by the Gestapo were starved and tortured. Many were executed. To carry out its brutal practices, the Gestapo recruited individuals who had no objection to cruelty. Emanuel Schafer, a senior Gestapo officer, was representative of the type of thug the Gestapo attracted. He was ambitious, ruthless, and had an insatiable appetite for violence. His hatred for Jews drew him to the Nazi Party, and during Hitler's rise Schafer served as one of his strong-arm men. On August 31, 1939, Schafer was part of the staged "attack" against Germany that Hitler used as an excuse to invade Poland and start World War II.

When Hitler's armies overran most of Europe, the Gestapo was right behind them. Nazi-occupied countries came under harsh military rule. The Gestapo forced men and teenage boys to go to Germany as slave labor. Members of the Resistance (groups that fought against the invaders) were hunted down and shot. Anyone suspected of being a spy for the Allies (British, Americans, and others who were united against Hitler) was arrested and subjected to vicious interrogation.

The Gestapo committed its worst atrocities against Jews all over Europe. They were transported to death camps like Auschwitz, where millions were murdered in gas chambers. Emanuel Schafer, who was in charge of Gestapo operations in Belgrade, Yugoslavia, boasted that he had rid the city of every single Jew.

The Gestapo terror ended with Germany's defeat in 1945. Captured Gestapo officers were put on trial as war criminals. Some were executed. Others, like Schafer, were sentenced to prison terms. But even after the Gestapo was gone, its legacy of secrecy and fear haunted Europe for many years.

The Gestapo was ruthless, and its methods were horrific. But the idea of such a cold-blooded instrument of fear and control

GESTAPO "MUG SHOTS"

As part of their propaganda campaign to portray Jews and other ethnic groups as "inferior," the Gestapo would photograph the faces of men who had been beaten, starved, and not allowed to shave for several days. The images made the men appear brutish. This was supposed to show the German people that Hitler's police were protecting them from criminals of the lowest sort.

wasn't new. Men like Hitler and Himmler took ideas from history when they formed their secretive organizations.

WATCHING EYES: FROM PALACE TO PEOPLE

Monarchs of bygone times were primarily concerned with plots being hatched in the ranks of the aristocracy. Their secret police spied on ambitious nobles and courtiers. King Henry VIII of 16th century England, for example, was suspicious of everybody in his court, and had eyes and ears everywhere. Henry had more people executed for "treason" than any other British monarch. Among those who lost their heads were several high-ranking nobles and two of Henry's six wives.

Perhaps the most famous case involving spies and royal intrigue was that of Mary, Queen of Scots, also in the 16th century. Scottish nobles had forced Mary to abdicate her throne, and she fled to England to seek the protection of her cousin, Queen Elizabeth I. However, Sir Francis Walsingham, the head of Queen Elizabeth's secret service organization, suspected that Mary wanted to seize the throne of England. His spies kept close watch on her for years, and even read all of her mail. Elizabeth eventually had Mary executed, after Walsingham convinced her that Mary was a serious threat to her rule.

Rarely, unless there was a popular rebellion, or somebody reported a person for seditious behavior, would a monarch think it necessary to send secret police out among the common people. Superstitious peasants simply held the "ruling class" in too much

awe. The people of some Asian countries regarded emperors as gods. In Europe, people believed kings and queens ruled by "divine right"—which meant their authority came from God.

However, as centuries passed and new ideas took root, people began to doubt the right of monarchs to hold absolute power. In some countries kings were deposed and even executed. Rulers now had to be concerned with what the common people were thinking and plotting. No one was more aware of that than Napoleon Bonaparte, the general who had emerged from the chaos of the French Revolution as ruler of France. In a nation that had just beheaded its king, Napoleon would need a wider network of secret police than earlier rulers would have ever imagined.

JOSEPH FOUCHÉ: THE CHAMELEON

On Christmas Eve in 1800, enemies of Napoleon attempted to assassinate him with a bomb as he rode in his coach to the Paris Opera. The explosion killed or wounded dozens of people, but Napoleon was unharmed. He ordered Joseph Fouché, his minister of police, to track down the conspirators.

A former schoolteacher, Fouché was ambitious, ruthless, and the most hated and feared man in France. He was described as a man with "a heart as hard as a diamond, a stomach of iron, and a tearless eye." Throughout the power struggles of the French Revolution, as heads tumbled from the guillotine, Fouché was a chameleon. He was always ready and able to change his colors and emerge on the winning side. There was no political group Fouché supported that he hadn't also betrayed. He had no personal loyalty to Napoleon. He served him because, for the moment, Napoleon was the most powerful man in France. Napoleon had made Fouché the country's minister of police because he was cunning, merciless, and coldly efficient. But he didn't entirely trust him.

FOUCHÉ'S BIGGEST SECRET

Napoleon didn't know that Joseph Fouché even had a secret file on *him*. It was stuffed with information Fouché had cleverly sifted from friendly conversations with an unsuspecting source: Napoleon's wife, Josephine.

Fouché had agents watching and listening everywhere, including in Napoleon's army. Many were criminals recruited from prisons. They were given the choice of going to the guillotine or working for the police. Fouché's men entrapped unsuspecting, innocent citizens

so they could be blackmailed into being his spies. They even spied on Napoleon's family. All of the information went into secret files known only to Fouché, who took pride in knowing what everybody was up to. Fouché boasted that in Paris, three men couldn't get together to talk without him knowing about it. That may have been an exaggeration, but for Fouché—and Napoleon—it was important that people *believed* it was true.

Fouché's police soon found the men responsible for the Christmas Eve plot. Then he turned the assassination attempt to Napoleon's advantage by using it as an excuse to get rid of many more of Napoleon's political enemies. Fouché rounded up dozens of people who'd had nothing to do with the plot. They were charged with treason and then executed or exiled.

Fouché kept his chameleon-like ways throughout Napoleon's eventful reign. When Napoleon was finally defeated and sent into exile in 1815, Fouché actually managed to become president of the commission that governed France. However, his past caught up to him and he was soon exiled to Italy, where he died in 1820. Fouché's secret police system had been so effective that his methods were studied by spymasters and dictators of later generations, including Adolf Hitler. Fouché has been called the architect of the modern police state.

THE TONTON MACOUTES: UNCLE GUNNYSACK

In the 19th and 20th centuries, many so-called "Third World" nations experienced violent upheavals due to unstable governments, weak economies, and social inequalities left over from colonialism. Attempts to establish democracies failed in the face of widespread poverty and official corruption. Discontent led to insurrections and civil wars. Sometimes a "strongman" rose up to take control of the government and the people. Very often he'd be a military officer who commanded the loyalty of the army. Nonetheless, he was an unelected dictator who governed through force.

To maintain their hold on power, these strongmen always employed secret police.

One such leader was Fulgencio Batista, dictator of Cuba. Batista had thousands of political dissenters killed, and was deeply involved with American Mafia bosses. He was overthrown in 1959 by Fidel Castro, who turned Cuba into a communist country and established his own force of secret police to deal with opponents.

Rafael Leonidas Trujillo, dictator of the Dominican Republic from 1930 until his assassination in 1961, presided over one of the most brutal regimes in Latin America. The Dominican people lived in terror of his National Guard and his secret police force, the Servicio de Inteligencia Militar (SIM). Besides keeping a close watch on the population, SIM and the National Guard spied on each other.

Augusto Pinochet ruled Chile with an iron fist from 1973 to 1981. His secret police force, the Directorate of National Intelligence (DINA), arrested more than eighty thousand men, women, and children. Many of them were tortured or murdered, or disappeared without a trace.

One person who survived an unexpected visit from secret police wrote an account of the harrowing experience. Dantès Bellegarde was in his home in the Haitian capital of Port-au-Prince one

CRIME REPORT

The Dominican people had to call Trujillo *El Jefe* (The Chief), and lived in fear of his secret police. You would be in trouble if they entered your home and you didn't have a photograph of *El Jefe* prominently displayed.

night in 1960 when the front door suddenly burst open and several armed men stormed in. At age eighty-two Bellegarde was a highly regarded historian and diplomat. That meant nothing to the intruders. The leader shoved a machine gun in Bellegarde's face and forced him up against a wall. He kept Bellegarde there, terrified, while the others tore through his library. They overturned bookshelves, ripped up papers and books, and yanked his telephone from the wall. When they were finished and the room was a shambles, the leader struck the old man on the face. Then they left. Not a word had been spoken.

Bellegarde knew who the men were. He knew that he was lucky they hadn't killed him, or worse, forced him to go with them. Terrible things happened to people who got taken away by the Tonton Macoutes, the secret police of Haiti's dictator, Dr. François Duvalier, better known as Papa Doc.

When Papa Doc took power in Haiti in 1957, he didn't trust the leaders of the Haitian army. He created a secret police force that was loyal only to him. Officially, this paramilitary organization

THE END OF "UNCLE GUNNYSACK"

Papa Doc died in 1971 and was succeeded by his son Jean-Claude (Baby Doc). Baby Doc was deposed in a popular uprising in 1986. Fearing reprisals, many Tonton Macoutes fled Haiti. Those who remained formed illegal militia units that continued to terrorize Haitians, but by 2000 their power had declined.

was called the Militia of National Security Volunteers. The Haitian people nicknamed them the Tonton Macoutes (Uncle Gunnysack) after a boogeyman of Haitian legend who stuffed disobedient children into a sack and carried them away.

Papa Doc ruled through brute force and terror. He didn't care if the impoverished people of Haiti despised him, as long as they feared him. The Haitians' dread of Papa Doc was almost supernatural, because he claimed to have strong powers of voodoo, a form of religious worship mixed with sorcery.

Tonton Macoutes spies were everywhere. Anyone who dared say a word against Papa Doc was arrested or mysteriously disappeared. No one could leave the country without permission. Even requesting permission could get you in trouble. The border with the neighboring Dominican Republic was heavily patrolled.

Papa Doc's family lived in the luxurious presidential palace. Beneath the palace was a dungeon. That was where the Tonton Macoutes interrogated and tortured prisoners, frequently with Papa Doc looking on. It was said that anyone who was taken there either talked or died— often both.

Papa Doc's ruthlessness knew no bounds. When students painted anti-Duvalier graffiti on walls in Port-au-Prince, the Tonton Macoutes rounded up thirty suspects. They were tortured and executed. When Haitian rebels shot and killed three Tonton Macoutes who were personal bodyguards of the Duvalier family, Papa Doc unleashed his private army in a vengeful vendetta. The Tonton Macoutes shot people down in the streets and in their homes. Most of the hundreds who were arrested were never seen again.

THE SOVIET UNION: THE KGB

In the Russian Revolution of 1917, Czar Nicholas II was overthrown. A communist regime led by Vladimir Lenin seized power and extended Russian control over numerous smaller countries. Together they formed a large political confederation called the Soviet Union. A secret police force called Cheka was formed to keep watch on the people. It would operate under several names until 1954, when it became known as the KGB. But whatever name it went by, the Soviet secret police force was an instrument for state-instituted terror. Lenin's successor, Josef Stalin, used it for "purges" that sent thousands of people to their deaths or to exile in Siberian labor camps.

CURTAIN OF FEAR

In a now-famous 1946 speech, British statesman Winston Churchill called the wall of secrecy around the Soviet Union and the Eastern Bloc an "Iron Curtain." For people living behind the Iron Curtain, secret police like the KGB were a chilling fact of life.

After World War II, Poland, East Germany, Hungary, Czechoslovakia, Bulgaria, and Romania were occupied by Stalin's Red Army. They were governed by puppet communist regimes under Soviet control. Each of them had a secret police force based on the Soviet model. One of the most notorious was the Securitate of Romanian dictator Nicolae Ceausescu. Under his brutal administration, the Securitate tortured and murdered thousands of people. High on the list of "enemies of the state" were writers, artists, scientists, teachers, university students, and anyone else considered an "intellectual" with anti-communist ideas.

Agents of the KGB, the Securitate, and other communist secret police departments spied on their own people, and engaged in espionage against the United States and its allies. Secret police lurked in every town and village, and were planted in embassies in foreign capitals. As in the dark days of the Nazi Gestapo, people lived in an atmosphere of fear and suspicion.

The Cold War ended in 1991 with the collapse of the Soviet Union. Even then, the cloak-and-dagger work of secret police continued. In one incident, a Russian secret service agent named Alexander Litvinenko uncovered evidence that his department had been involved in terrorist acts. He fled to the United Kingdom. On November 1, 2006, shortly after meeting two former Russian agents,

Litvinenko fell ill. He died a few weeks later from poisoning by radioactive polonium-210, which had probably been slipped into his tea. Doctors called the assassination "the beginning of an era of nuclear terrorism."

The former KGB is now the Russian Foreign Intelligence Service. It is answerable to the Russian federal government—unlike the KGB, which was practically a law unto itself.

NATIONAL SECURITY

Almost every nation has a police organization that, for the purposes of national security, operates out of the public eye. In addition to monitoring the activities of international drug and arms smugglers as well as terrorists, these police forces are responsible for monitoring foreign espionage, or spying. In many cases they engage in espionage against countries they consider a threat, though even friendly countries have been targets. Not surprisingly, revelations about such "friendly" surveillance often cause serious diplomatic rifts.

In the United States, domestic secret police work is carried out by the FBI. Foreign surveillance and intelligence gathering is conducted by the Central Intelligence Agency (CIA). The British counterparts to the American secret police organizations are MI5 and MI6. Israel's secret police organization, Mossad, has had the additional task of tracking down Nazi war criminals. Various reports allege that Mossad has undertaken targeted killings in clandestine operations.

During the Cold War, the CIA and MI5 were primarily engaged in a "spy versus spy" conflict with the KGB. One of the most dramatic incidents occurred in 1949, when British agents suspected that MI5 had been infiltrated by a "mole," an enemy spy planted in their organization. The investigative trail eventually led to a German scientist codenamed "Rest" who had been working with the Americans and British on secret atomic research as an MI5 operative, and was passing classified information to the Soviets. The spy was arrested, tried, and sentenced to a long prison term.

More recently, the CIA, MI5, and the secret services of other Western nations and allies have been involved in the fight against terrorist organizations like the Middle East–based al Qaeda. Motivated by political and religious idealism, al Qaeda has claimed responsibility for numerous bombings and assassinations. Its most horrific atrocity was the September 11, 2001, attacks that resulted in the destruction of New York's World Trade Center; major damage to the Pentagon in Arlington County, Virginia; the crash of an airliner in Pennsylvania; and the loss of almost three thousand lives.

The CIA undertook a long and meticulous hunt for Osama bin Laden, the founder of al Qaeda and the terrorist behind the 9/11 tragedy. After nearly ten years, agents finally located his hideout in Pakistan. On May 2, 2011, a special team striking out of a CIA base in Afghanistan raided the compound and killed bin Laden in an operation codenamed "Neptune Spear."

Although bin Laden's killing was considered a just action by the CIA and the American public in general, Operation Neptune Spear raised many questions. Among other concerns, the government of Pakistan complained that the Americans had violated their

THE ORIGIN OF 007

Author Ian Fleming worked for the British Secret Service during World War II. He later used a real secret agent as the model for his most famous literary creation, MI6's James Bond.

national sovereignty. The American government responded that the operation required the utmost secrecy or bin Laden might have been warned and allowed to escape. That response implied that the Americans didn't think Pakistani officials were trustworthy.

The questions of when, how, and to what extent government security agencies should be allowed to operate in secrecy form an ongoing debate. Defenders of secret police insist that secrecy is necessary in the fight against terrorism. They make the argument that citizens who are doing nothing wrong have nothing to worry about.

However, civil rights advocates make strong objections against the invasion of privacy and the potential oppression that so often accompany these investigations. Privacy is of particular concern in this modern age of super-spy technology that allows secret service organizations to not only watch people from satellites and tap into telephone conversations, but also to hack into computers and read private emails. Security organizations even search social media sites and Internet chatrooms for "red flags"—information that might place a person under suspicion.

Although national security police certainly have to keep much of their work quiet and undercover if they are to be effective, many people believe there have to be limits. Their argument goes back to the time of Napoleon and Joseph Fouché: democratically elected governments have a duty to ensure that citizens' civil liberties are respected, and not violated for the sake of secrecy.

CHAPTER 10

POLICE TODAY

JUST AS INVENTIONS LIKE THE AUTOMOBILE AND THE TELEPHONE revolutionized law enforcement in the 20th century, amazing technological advances have changed policing in the 21st century. Police now use electronic communications and surveillance systems linked by satellite. Police stations and police cars are computerized. New scientific techniques have not only enhanced the recovery of finger, hand, and foot prints, but have added ear and lip printing to the investigator's tool kit. A forensic artist can reconstruct a face for an unidentified skull. An autopsy can reveal volumes of information about a body, and sometimes

ETHNIC DIVERSITY

Adapting police personnel to community changes resulting from immigration is a common and long-standing practice. In the 19th and 20th centuries, police departments in North America found it advantageous to recruit officers from many minority ethnic groups. Black, Italian, Irish, Polish, Hispanic, and Jewish officers were among those who contributed to the cosmopolitan makeup of police forces, and the respective communities benefited. The trend continues in the 21st century, as police departments welcome people from even more diverse backgrounds.

ON CAMERA

First developed in 1976, but technologically enhanced in the 21st century, Automated Number Plate Recognition systems can scan the license plates of vehicles traveling at 100 kmph (62 mph) at the rate of one per second.

about a murderer. Most remarkable of all has been the DNA breakthrough.

But even in this high-tech age, some old-style policing methods are still useful. Mounted police officers still patrol big city parks. K9 units (dogs) can be an officer's best friend in sniffing out hidden drugs and explosives, and in tracking down suspects and fugitives. Police on bicycles can reach places inaccessible to cars.

POLICE AROUND THE WORLD

Police departments and duties vary from country to country. In Japan, for example, streets are patrolled by officers called *Omawarisan*. This roughly translates as "Mr. Honorable Walking Around," although the officers actually use bicycles and motor scooters. Like the English bobbies, they work out of neighborhood police stations and are part of community life. In Tokyo, a city of more than 13 million people, nobody is more than a fifteen-minute walk from the nearest *koban* (police station). Officers are so in touch with the pulse of local life that neighborhoods in this metropolis are among the safest in the world.

China has the world's largest number of police, with over 2 million officers divided between two main departments. The Ministry of State Security enforces oppressive government measures to control the population. It watches people for political dissent, and monitors the activities of visiting foreigners. In fact, China is regularly accused of human rights violations for imprisoning citizens without trial. The much larger People's Armed Police Force deals with criminal matters and domestic responsibilities such as

THE POPE'S POLICE

The famous Swiss Guards at the Vatican are responsible for the pope's protection, but this tiny independent state in the middle of Rome also has its own police. The Gendarmerie Corps of Vatican City State, which has 130 members, is a uniformed police force that carries out general police duties such as traffic control and criminal investigations. To join this police force, a recruit must be an unmarried Roman Catholic male.

fire regulations. In Chinese cities, local police stations maintain registries of all community residents and visitors. They keep files on births, deaths, marriages, and divorces, and officers conduct random household checks.

The tiny Mediterranean nation of Monaco, with thirty-five thousand people, has 515 police officers. That makes it the most heavily policed country in the world on the basis of population and geographic area. Over a hundred of the officers belong to an elite unit that protects the prince of Monaco and his palace. Monaco has such a strong police presence because it is one of the wealthiest countries in Europe. Its location on the French Riviera and its grand casino are attractions for the rich and famous, making the nation a tempting target for criminals.

Some countries have laws against activities that would not be considered criminal elsewhere. In Saudi Arabia, police called *Mutaween* enforce a strict religious code. Among other things, it forbids people to adopt certain aspects of Western culture such as clothing and music.

In Singapore, for purposes of public sanitation, chewing gum is prohibited unless the gum is prescribed by a doctor for therapeutic purposes. If you live in Thailand, you are not allowed to leave your home without wearing underwear, and it is illegal to step on the national currency.

DO YOU WANT TO BE A POLICE OFFICER?

Policing can be an exciting and challenging career that offers many possibilities. You can drive a patrol car and answer 9-1-1 calls, solve crimes as a detective, work as a traffic-collision reconstructionist, or be a forensic computer technician who retrieves deleted evidence. The number and variety of jobs is constantly growing. However, as much as modern technology has changed policing, one thing it has not replaced is the social skill required for face-to-face interaction between police officers and the public.

Young people considering a career in policing today must meet stricter requirements than those of a century ago. Rules vary from country to country, but many of them are basically the same world-wide. All police officers must be citizens of the country in which they are employed.

Most police departments require applicants to have at least a high-school diploma or the equivalent. Many prefer potential recruits to have a college or university degree. In some places it's to the applicant's advantage to know a second language.

Most recruits attend some form of police academy for training. In addition to learning the law and policing skills, cadets also learn

first aid and CPR (cardiopulmonary resuscitation). Cadets must
pass an examination to graduate from the academy. Once they are
accepted by a police department, new officers undergo about two
months of on-the-job "coaching" with veteran officers.

In the United States, some police departments offer programs
designed to introduce young people to the realities of police work.
They can participate in various volunteer projects, and accompany
officers on ride-alongs that give them a firsthand look at a cop's
working day. For instance, the Los Angeles County Sheriff's Department's Explorer Program allows aspiring deputies to participate in
patrols, help at DUI (driving under the influence) checkpoints, and
assist the beach team at Malibu.

Recruiters have found that many young applicants have misconceptions about policing that come from movies and TV shows. They want to start right off as detectives, or they expect daily adventures full of car chases and confrontations with armed criminals. Recruiters emphasize that TV shows and movies are rarely realistic.

Applicants to a police academy or institution must provide solid references and be willing to undergo thorough background checks to ensure they have a clean record and are well suited to the job. They must also participate in logical and psychological testing. Such tests are good indicators of an applicant's mental and emotional fitness for the job, but are never 100 percent accurate. A police cadet will face further "checks" along the way.

IT'S NOT ALL GUNS AND CAR CHASES

An important part of a police officer's job involves sitting at a desk writing reports. It might seem tedious, but officers have to keep careful records of their work. Sometimes they have to testify in court, and the details in their evidence can can be crucial to a criminal conviction.

Even after cadets graduate and become police officers, their performance is scrutinized to ensure that they remain physically and mentally capable of working at a high level of efficiency. This monitoring is also a safeguard against unlawful police behavior. (Police officers who break the law face disciplinary action and can even be dismissed from the force and prosecuted.) In many police departments, officers have a training day within their station every four to six weeks, and annual training and re-qualification in a police college or similar facility.

Police work can be stressful, especially when it involves violent and unpredictable people. Many officers say that the real stress does not occur at the moment of a confrontation, because their instincts and training help them deal with that. Instead, it comes later, when the emotional impact of what just happened settles in, and the officer has to justify whatever steps were taken in the situation. Often, an officer cannot talk about job-related experiences with family members, because it would be too gruesome, inappropriate, or emotional to share. Police work also requires confidentiality, so it's not possible in many instances to share information about cases.

Being a police officer means making personal sacrifices, such as putting in extra time when necessary, sometimes without notice. This can place an added burden on what is already a high-stress occupation. Officers have to learn how to maintain a healthy balance between family life and the responsibilities of their job.

Society's need for police evolves, but never ceases. As long as people are governed by laws, there will be a demand for people to uphold those laws. Police departments will always recruit bright, enthusiastic young applicants. The pay and other benefits are attractive, and there are many challenging fields within law enforcement to explore.

In some places, a police officer who has served for twenty-five years is eligible to retire from the force with a pension. Some veteran officers take advantage of this and go into business for themselves. They are often in demand in the growing field of private, industrial, and corporate security.

THE PERILS OF POLICE WORK

Above all, police officers and their families have to live with the knowledge that policing can be very dangerous work. A routine shift can end suddenly with a serious injury, and some officers die in the line of duty. No one can say how many law enforcement officers have died in the line of duty worldwide throughout the centuries. Records from the earliest times are sketchy, and for some places nonexistent.

Firearms in the hands of criminals and and people with mental health issues have been by far the greatest cause of death and serious injury to police officers, especially in the United States. Accidents involving automobiles and other vehicles are a distant second. Many officers have died by drowning, fire, explosions, and electrocution while carrying out hazardous rescue operations. Some have died in training accidents; still others have succumbed to duty-related illnesses. These are the risks men and women accept when they decide to become police officers.

CONCLUSION

FROM THE SCYTHIAN ARCHERS OF ANCIENT ATHENS TO THE modern world of Interpol and the FBI, police have played an important role in the development of societies and the establishment of the rule of law. Peasant posses and nobles like Sir Robert Colville helped suppress banditry in the Middle Ages. Chinese investigators introduced the world to forensic science. Joseph Fouché showed how police could be the agents of a despotic ruler, and Sir Robert Peel instituted policing as a profession represented by a community's "finest."

Over the centuries, police officers have been slaves, soldiers, warriors, knights, gardeners, and gunfighters. They have walked the dark streets of London and ridden the vast open prairies of Canada. Some, like Superintendent Leonard Read of Scotland Yard and Frank Serpico of the New York City Police Department, have been heroes. Others have been tainted by corruption, or have even, like the Nazi Gestapo, acted as agents of terror. Policing has evolved from a male-dominated profession to one in which women are now firmly established within forces. Today constables rely more on brains than muscle, and their profession is as much about preventing crime as it is about reacting to it.

Right now, in your own community, police officers are controlling traffic, walking beats, and patrolling highways. Somewhere a uniformed officer is responding to a call about an assault, investigating a human trafficking operation, or developing a criminal profile, while elsewhere a plainclothes detective is questioning a witness about a burglary. While our image of police work is often defined by television shows and movies, it isn't always about dramatic chases or heated interrogations. Many police work quietly behind the scenes, while others are more visible in our everyday life. No matter the task, this wide range of police functions is critical to a healthy society, and to a world in which order is preserved and our communities are safe.

GLOSSARY

Apartheid: the South African system of officially separating the white, black, and Asian populations

Ballistics: the mechanical science that deals with the behavior, flight, and effects of projectiles, particularly bullets

Bertillon System: a criminal identification system employing photographs and body measurements, developed by Alphonse Bertillon of France in 1870

Cohortes urbanes (urban cohorts): the police force instituted by Roman emperor Caesar Augustus in the first century BCE

Coroner: from an archaic French word for crown (corouner). In medieval times the coroner represented the monarch in all legal matters. Today the coroner's primary duty is to investigate any death thought to be of other than natural causes.

Espionage: the secret watching of another; spying

Extradition: the transfer of a fugitive or criminal from one jurisdiction to another

DUI: driving under the influence (of alcohol or drugs)

Forensics: the use of science and technology to investigate and establish facts in a criminal case

Hue and cry: loud shouts made to alert others during the pursuit of a criminal

Kapu: the legal and religious code of native Hawaiians in pre-colonial times. Kapu was abolished under European influence, but some of the symbols of kapu are still in use.

Krypteia: secret police who kept watch over enslaved helots in ancient Sparta between 700 and 400 BCE

Lynch: to hang or otherwise execute a suspected criminal without due process of law

National security: the measures taken by a state to ensure its survival and safety

Odontology: the branch of science that deals with the study of teeth

Poaching: hunting and fishing illegally

Posse comitatus **(posse):** a body of men called upon to serve the state, usually in the pursuit of a criminal

Prohibition: an American law of the early 20th century that forbade the manufacture and sale of alcoholic beverages

Shire reeve: in medieval England, an officer who presided over a shire. Origin of the word *sheriff*.

Streltsy: the soldier-police of Moscow, between 1550 and 1700

Surveillance: a close watch, supervision

Vigilante: one who takes or advocates the taking of law enforcement into one's own hands

Vigiles urbani **(urban watchmen):** a combination police and fire department that patrolled the streets of ancient Rome at night

TIMELINE

Prehistory	Early societies establish rules of cooperation, enforced by chiefs, elders, and warriors
c. 1772 BCE	Hammurabi of Babylon writes the first known code of law
c. 500 BCE	Scythian Archers become police in Athens
c. 300 BCE	Kautilya establishes a police system in India
c. 220 BCE	Chinese prefects use forensics in criminal investigations
27 BCE	Caesar Augustus institutes the *cohortes urbanes* to police the streets of Rome
c. 1000 CE	European monarchs appoint nobles as justices of the peace
c. 1100	The county sheriff becomes the principal law enforcement officer in medieval England
1192	Beginning of the first shogunate in Japan; samurai warriors enforce laws
1383	King Fernando I founds Portugal's first police force, the *quadrilheiros*
1453	Sultan Mehmed II of the Ottoman Empire makes his gardeners, the *bastancis*, his police force
c. 1550	*Streltsy* police the streets of Moscow
1580	Towns in Elizabethan England are patrolled by the Watch
1650	Dutch citizens and police cooperate to make their cities the safest in Europe, and the newly invented streetlight helps reduce crime

1667	Nicolas de la Reynie, lieutenant governor of Paris, founds the world's first "modern" urban police department
1749	Henry Fielding establishes the Bow Street Runners, London's first professional police force
1799	Napoleon makes Joseph Fouché minister of police
1812	The world's first police detective force, the Sûreté Nationale, is established in Paris
1829	Sir Robert Peel's "Peelers" first appear on London streets. They will later be called "bobbies"
1842	Eight officers become the original "Detective Force" of Britain's Scotland Yard
1843	Belgian police take the first criminal "mugshots"
1870	Alphonse Bertillon develops a system of criminal identification using photographs and body measurements
1873	The Canadian government founds the North West Mounted Police
1888	Dr. Thomas Bond produces the first example of criminal profiling
1891	Police in Argentina are the first to use fingerprint evidence to convict a murderer
1899	The first police car, with an electric motor, is used in Akron, Ohio
1919	The New York City Police Department is the first in the world to acquire aircraft
1923	The International Criminal Police Commission (ICPC) is founded

1923	Police in Victoria, Australia, are the first to use a car radio—a one-way system that allows officers in the car to receive messages, but not send them
1924	The United States Congress authorizes a national fingerprint file
1925	Two Americans, Philip Gravelle and Calvin Goddard, invent the comparison microscope, which is used for matching bullet markings
1933	Bayonne, New Jersey, police use the first two-way car radio
1934	Americans experiment in cooperative crime control with the Five State Pac
1935	The Bureau of Investigation officially becomes the Federal Bureau of Investigation (FBI)
1939–45	European nations under German occupation are terrorized by the Gestapo, the Nazi secret police
1946	British police are the first to use a helicopter in a manhunt
1949	British police use dental remains and a gallstone to convict serial killer John Haigh
1954	Robert Borkenstein, an American, invents the Breathalyzer, which can determine a person's blood alcohol content
1957	Dr. François "Papa Doc" Duvalier takes power in Haiti and forms the Tonton Macoutes
1968	The American federal government encourages police departments to computerize; by the early 1970s, most American police departments have computers
1970	Frank Serpico exposes corruption in the New York City Police Department

1974	Start of Britain's Police National Computer (PNC), which is accessible to law enforcement agencies across the U.K. twenty-four hours a day
1986	British police are the first to use DNA to solve a criminal case
1993	Kirk Bloodsworth, an American who has served eight years in prison, is the first person to have a murder conviction overturned on DNA evidence
1995	The world's first DNA database is established in Britain, storing DNA profiles from all convicted criminals
On into the 21st century	Police departments use social media to investigate crimes, police departments experiment with new technology such as unmanned surveillance drones and Google Glass (a computer that is worn like eyeglasses)

BIBLIOGRAPHY

PRINT SOURCES

Brooks, Stephen. "The Murder of Rio's Street Kids," *Insight Magazine*, August 5, 1991.

Butts, Edward. *The Desperate Ones: Forgotten Canadian Outlaws*. Toronto: Dundurn, 2006.

Connolly, Peter. *The Ancient City: Life in Classical Athens and Rome*. Oxford, U.K.: Oxford University Press, 1998.

Cruise, David, and Alison Griffiths. *The Great Adventure: How the Mounties Conquered the West*. Toronto: Penguin Books, 1997.

Das, Sukla. *Crime and Punishment in Ancient India*. New Delhi: Abhinav Publishers, 1977.

Gernet, Jacques. *A History of Chinese Civilization*. Cambridge, U.K.: Cambridge University Press, 1982.

Gleimus, Nita, Evelina Sibanyoni, and Emma Mthimunye. *First Peoples of Africa: The Zulu*. Minneapolis, MN: Lerner Publications Co., 2003.

Grudgings, Stuart. "Rio Police Accused of Death Squad Killings," Reuters, July 7, 2009.

Heinl, Robert Debs and Nancy Gordon Heinl. *Written in Blood: The Story of the Haitian People*, 1492–1971. Boston: Houghton Mifflin Company, 1978.

Hussey, Andrew. *Paris: The Secret History*. New York: Bloomsbury Press, 2006.

Israel, Jonathan. *The Dutch Republic: Its Rise, Greatness, and Fall: 1477–1806*, Oxford, U.K.: Clarendon Press, 1995.

Keen, Maurice. *The Outlaws of Medieval England*. Abingdon, U.K.: Routledge, 2000.

Kendall, Ann. *Everyday Life of the Incas*. New York: Dorset Press, 1973.

Keneally, Thomas. *Australians: Origins to Eureka*. Crows Nest, NSW, Australia: Allen & Unwin, 2009.

Leeder, Jessica. "Now Someone Will Kill Me," *Globe & Mail*, Toronto, November 1, 2008.

Lewis, Mark Edward. *The Early Chinese Empires, Qin and Han*. Cambridge, MA: Belknap Press of Harvard University Press, 2007.

Marks, Paula Mitchell. *And Die in the West: The Story of the OK Corral Gunfight*. New York: William Morrow and Company Inc., 1989.

McQuail, Lisa. *First Peoples of Africa: The Masai*. Minneapolis, MN: Lerner Publications Co., 2002.

Mortimer, Ian. *The Time Traveler's Guide to Medieval England*. New York: Touchstone Books, 2008.

Perkins, Dorothy. *Encyclopedia of Japan*. New York: Roundtable Press Books, 1991.

Rogow, Sally M. *Faces of Courage: Young Heroes of World War II*. Vancouver: Granville Island Publishing, 2003.

Singman, Jeffrey L. *Daily Life in Elizabethan England*. Westport, CT: Greenwood Press, 1995.

Sturtevant, William C. (general ed.). *Handbook of North American Indians, Volumes 8 & 15*. Washington, DC: The Smithsonian Institute, 1978.

Walker, Samuel and Charles Katz. *The Police In America: An Introduction*. New York: McGraw-Hill Higher Education, 2012.

Weaver, Muriel Porter. *The Aztecs, Maya, and Their Predecessors*. Orlando, FL: Academic Press, 1981.

Wheatcroft, Andrew. *The Ottomans*. London: Viking, 1993.

ONLINE SOURCES

A History of Policing in Toronto: "Equal Partners." Toronto Policing website. Retrieved from www.torontopolice.on.ca/publications/files/misc/history/.

Blackwell, Tom. "Afghan Woman Police Director Gunned Down by Taliban," Rawa News, September 28, 2009. Retrieved from http://www.rawa.org/temp/runews/2008/09/28/afghan-woman-police-director-gunned-down-by-taliban.html.

Creative Spirits. "Australia Tribal Punishment, Customary Law & Payback." Retrieved from www.creativespirits.info/aboriginalculture/law/tribal-punishment-customary-law-payback.

Feminist Majority Foundation. "A History of Women in Policing." Retrieved from http://womenandpolicing.com/history/historytext.htm.

Free Information Society. "Serpico, Frank." Retrieved from "http://www.freeinfosociety.com/article.php?id=402" www.freeinfosociety.com/article.php?id=402.

International Association of Women Police: www.iawp.org

International Centre for the History of Crime, Policing, and Justice. "The Women Police: The First Women Police Officers." Retrieved from www.open.ac.uk/Arts/history-from-police-archives/Met6Kt/WomenPolice/wpFwp.html.

Kerala Police History & Archives. "History of Police in India." Retrieved from HYPERLINK "http://www.keralapolicehistory.com/hist1.html" www.keralapolicehistory.com/hist1.html.

Metropolitan Police Service (London). "Women in the Police." Retrieved from content.met.police.uk/Article/Women-in-the-Police/1400015656544/1400015656544.

Police Federation of Australia. "Australia National Police Memorial." Retrieved from www.npm.org.au.

INDEX

ACKNOWLEDGMENTS

The author would like to thank the following individuals and institutions for their wonderful assistance in providing material for this book, helping with research, or contributing to its preparation: Media Relations Officer Victor Kwong of the Metropolitan Toronto Police Services; Inspector Julia Jaeger, Metropolitan Police, UK (retired); PCs Kate Peplow, Cathy Morgan, and Diana Shaw, Birmingham City Police; Carol Paterick, Libby Lytle; Trudy Lewis, Arlington, Texas, Police Department; the staff at Annick Press, Pam Robertson, Linda Pruessen, the International Association of Women Police, the helpful members of www.gangsterologists.com, and as always the staff at the Public Library in Guelph, Ontario.

ABOUT THE AUTHOR AND ILLUSTRATOR

ED BUTTS loved history and adventure stories as a kid, and started writing short stories, articles, and poetry in his teens. On rare occasions when a magazine published his work, he was overjoyed, especially when they sent him a check for ten dollars.

Since then, Ed has written books about explorers, adventurers, criminals, hidden treasure, disasters, mysteries, and daring women. He has also worked at many other jobs, including teaching at a school in the Dominican Republic for eight years.

Ed lives in Guelph, Ontario, with his daughter and grandson.

GARETH WILLIAMS is a mostly self-taught artist who lives in Kempton Park, South Africa. He started drawing at about three years of age and hasn't stopped since. Before settling on illustration, he dreamed of a career as a professional cricketer, and playing drums in a rock band.

Gareth has illustrated several books published in South Africa, as well as *The Adventures of Medical Man*, and *Outlaws, Spies, and Gangsters*.